THE EARLY PAPACY

ADRIAN FORTESCUE

THE EARLY PAPACY
to the Synod of Chalcedon in 451

Fourth Edition Edited by
Alcuin Reid

IGNATIUS PRESS   SAN FRANCISCO

✝

First edition published by
Burns, Oates and Washbourne
London, © 1920

Cover art:
Saint Peter receiving the keys from Jesus
Enamel plaque from a reliquary or altar. England, ca. 1180–1185.
Musee des Beaux-Arts, Dijon, France
© Erich Lessing/Art Resource, New York

Cover design by Roxanne Mei Lum

ISBN 978-1-58617-176-6
Library of Congress Control Number 2007927188
Printed in the United States of America ⊗

CONTENTS

INTRODUCTION

Adrian Fortescue was born on January 14, 1874. His father was an Anglican clergyman who was received into the Catholic Church in 1871 and who died in 1877.[1] Adrian was educated by the Jesuits at Boulougne-sur-Mer, and at St. Charles' College, Bayswater. In 1891 he entered the Scots' College in Rome, moving to the Faculty of Theology at Innsbrück University after three years. He was awarded a Ph.D. in Rome in 1894. His spare time was spent traveling and studying various ancient and modern languages, pleasures that became lasting passions.

Ordained a priest by Simon, Prince Bishop of Brixen, at Brixen, on Passion Sunday (March 27) 1898, he completed his studies at Innsbrück the following year. Having passed doctoral examinations in dogma and moral theology, Dr. Fortescue accepted a curacy at the German church in Whitechapel, London. After another curacy in Walthamstow, he was appointed rector of St. Helen's, Chipping Ongar, in 1901, returning to Innsbrück in May 1902 for further examinations in Church history, canon law and Arabic. Fortescue resigned his parish later that year, being unable personally to bear the burden of its finances.

---

[1] The baptistery chapel of the Church of St. Dominic, Haverstock Hill, London, was endowed by the Fortescue family and includes a memorial to Adrian and to his father, Edward Bowles Knottesford Fortescue.

During subsequent assignments in Colchester, White-chapel, Enfield, Witham and Maldon, Dr. Fortescue pre-pared for further examinations in Sacred Scripture and Hebrew; and for his final examination for the prestigious degree of Doctor of Divinity, to which he proceeded in 1905, he sub-mitted a thesis on St. John's authorship of the fourth Gospel.

Returning to England from a sabbatical year in Syria (1906–1907), he was appointed founding rector of the Cath-olic parish of Letchworth in Hertfordshire. Here the priest, scholar and extraordinarily gifted man that was Adrian Fortes-cue flourished. The parish of St. Hugh was a gem, care-fully polished by its founding pastor. However, the life of its devoted father was to end all too soon. He died at the age of forty-nine, on February 11, 1923, following an oper-ation for cancer.[2]

In 1919 in the columns of the *Tablet*, Fortescue vigor-ously defended the Catholic faith in the divinely instituted office of the papacy as integral to the Church founded by Jesus Christ. Fortescue wrote as an apologist for "the papal claims", particularly in the light of the equally vigorous rejec-tion of these by some of his non-Catholic contemporaries. Fortescue collected and revised these articles for publica-tion as a book in 1920.

His forthright style admits of little exception. Reading his work so many years later may at first give rise to con-cern. In our age, marked by the advance of ecumenism where the tendency is to speak, not of "non-Catholics",

---

[2] J. G. Vance and J. W. Fortescue wrote *Adrian Fortescue: A Memoir* (Lon-don: Burns, Oates and Washbourne, 1924), as a tribute following his death. More recently the late Michael Davies compiled *The Wisdom of Adrian Fortes-cue* (Fort Collins, Colo.: Roman Catholic Books, 1999), which contains fur-ther biographical information and extracts from his writings on the Sacred Liturgy.

but of "separated brethren" or of those in "real but imperfect communion" with the Church, it is not the done thing to emphasize that which sadly divides Christians. Yet the Catholic Church cannot renounce the papacy. That many followers of Christ in fact do to this day means that there is disagreement over something fundamental. Attempts to resolve this division are to be welcomed.

Reading Dr. Fortescue's clear exposition of the faith of the early Church in the papacy today may serve this end. And it may serve to increase the reader's knowledge of the Fathers of the Church up to 451.[3] It may even, please God, serve to assist some Christians to seek full communion with the Catholic Church.

In his 1995 encyclical letter *Ut unum sint* the late Pope John Paul II invited "dialogue" on the subject of the exercise of the office of the Bishop of Rome in an attempt to heal the divisions between the churches.[4] Any such dialogue must be informed by a sound knowledge of the Church's teaching on the papacy. *The Early Papacy* will be of assistance here.

Fortescue wrote within fifty years of the apotheosis of papal authority that is evidenced in the decree of the First

---

[3] Fr. Fortescue wrote in 1919, and since then, there have been advances in the study of patristics, none of which calls into question any of the texts adduced.

[4] See paragraph 96. In the previous paragraph, Pope John Paul II states that he desired to "find a way of exercising the primacy which, while in no way renouncing what is essential to its mission, is nonetheless open to a new situation". He also refers to his homily of December 6, 1987, delivered in the presence of the Ecumenical Patriarch of Constantinople, in which he said: "I insistently pray the Holy Spirit to shine his light upon us, enlightening all the Pastors and theologians of our Churches, that we may seek—together, of course—the forms in which this ministry may accomplish a service of love recognized by all concerned."

Vatican Council entitled *Pastor aeternus*. His period displayed a tendency to accord an uncritical obedience or even an exaggerated importance to the papacy. Given the widespread undermining of religious certainty in the wake of the so-called Enlightenment, and, in our own day, the internal turmoil faced by Western Catholicism, such a leaning somewhat more heavily on the rock of Peter is an understandable reaction.

It is, nevertheless, a reaction. As such it ought to be examined critically in order to guard against the dangerous error of ultramontanism. The belief that all juridical acts of the papacy, or that the policies or personal preferences of individual Popes have always been, are today, or always shall be right, is erroneous. Our Lord did not promise this to St. Peter and to his successors.

Our age, however, is characterized—nay, blighted—by the existence of those *within* the Catholic Church who deny or diminish the papacy's legitimate authority to govern the Church[5] or to teach with the authority of Christ in matters of faith and morals. Dr. Fortescue would curtly dismiss such "woolly thinking" in colorful words to the effect that, regardless of appearances, such persons had, to the extent that they had knowingly and willingly rejected this truth of the faith, long since ceased to be Catholic. It is one thing personally to disagree with the opinions or policies of a Pope (Fortescue taught his parishioners that "there had been very bad popes and foolish popes" and that they "were not bound to admire [Popes'] characters or believe

---

[5] Hans Urs von Balthasar wrote his book *The Office of Peter and the Structure of the Church* (San Francisco: Ignatius Press, 1986) precisely in response to this "deep-seated anti-Roman attitude".

their opinions").[6] But it is quite another thing still to deny or dissent from his authoritative teaching.[7]

Almost ironically, Fortescue's personal correspondence often caricatures and, on occasion, criticizes Popes and the papacy. He could even make light of having a portrait of the Pope:

> They[8] have given me a picture of a gentleman whom I recognise as that illustrious prelate the present incumbent of the Roman bishoprick [*sic*]: I am informed that if I look at it in the proper spirit it will give the pontifical blessing—a striking sight which I am naturally anxious to enjoy. Hitherto I have not succeeded in convincing it of my spiritual propriety. I have told it all the things that I think it would like to hear, that I am dead nuts on Encyclicals, that *ubi Petrus ibi* the whole show, that *Roma locuta est* (she never stops) *nulla salus est* (I hope I haven't got this mixed); I have even said polite things about its . . . predecessors of the X & XVth centuries; alas in vain! It hasn't once burst into *Sit nome Domini benedittumme* [*sic*].[9]

---

[6] Sermon on July 6, 1908, in "Notes of Sermons Preached by the Rev. Adrian Fortescue, Ph.D., D.D.", p. 3; typescript held in the Local Studies collection of the Letchworth Library.

[7] It must also be said, as Fr. Fortescue explains in chapter 2, that no matter how much one may (even rightly) be critical of a Pope's judgment or polices in matters not involving faith or morals, one cannot deny his right to command in ecclesiastical matters and the duty of Catholics to obey his commands. Clearly the principles of moral theology apply in the case of one who conscientiously believes that he cannot or ought not obey. Cf. further: G. Grisez, *The Way of the Lord Jesus*, vol. 1, *Christian Moral Principles* (Chicago: Franciscan Herald Press, 1983), especially chapter 11.

[8] The nuns in his parish, whom Fortescue styles the "little pink daughters of the penitent thief".

[9] Letter, September 20, 1902, St. Edmund's College Archive [hereafter SEC] 20–22–24. Letters from the St. Edmund's College Archive are quoted with the kind permission of the president.

Concerning antipapal reactionaries, he wrote:

> I hear about poor Tyrell and Modernism from everybody I
> speak to now. It occurs to me that most of these people
> start from a fundamental principle that, if the Pope is down
> on any mortal thing, that thing must be right. I believe that
> if Rome condemned highway robbery or wholesale adul-
> tery, pious Protestants would begin to think that there is a
> good deal to be said for them.[10]

Regarding the imposition of the antimodernist oath, he stated:

> We have stuck out for our position all our lives—unity,
> authority, St. Peter the rock and so on. I have too, and
> believe it; I am always preaching that sort of thing, and yet
> is it not now getting to a *reductio ad absurdum*? Centralisa-
> tion grows and goes madder every century. Even at Trent
> they hardly foresaw this kind of thing. Does it really mean
> that one cannot be a member of the Church of Christ with-
> out being, as we are, absolutely at the mercy of an Italian
> lunatic?
>   ... Give us back the Xth century Johns and Stephens, or
> a Borgia! They were less disastrous than this deplorable
> person.[11]

Writing to a friend about to travel to Rome, he observed:

---

[10] Letter, Dom. XXV post. Pent. 1907, SEC 20–22–45.

[11] Letter, November 5, 1910, SEC 20–22–66. The full text of this extremely
personal letter manifests Fortescue's acutely sensitive conscience, his intelli-
gence and his fidelity and orthodoxy as a Catholic priest. In this he perse-
vered faithfully until his death. His colorful opinions extracted above come
from a strictly private letter and are included here to illustrate the exasper-
ation that the policies of one (saintly) Pope could arouse in the most faithful
of priests. It is nevertheless true that Dr. Fortescue was no fan of St. Pius X;
cf. his manuscript letter of February 27, 1912, to Mrs. M. Crickmer.

There are a lot of fine things in the cities around, the Castelli romani [sic], especially Frascati, Marino, Lariccia, Castel Gandolfo, Genzano, Grottaferrata. What is left of the old Roman life is to be found in these. They represent still, more or less, what Rome would be if generations of Popes had not destroyed it, systematically, expensively, thoroughly.... Remember me to the present Ordinary, if you see him. I am told he is a decent man. It was Leo XIII in my time.[12]

On the activity of the Pontifical Biblical Commission, he wrote:

Time was when I was young and had no sense, *regnante Leone*, that I meant to read the Bible. The various decisions of the Pontifical Biblical Commission have long shown me that Christians had better leave that interesting volume altogether alone. Apparently there is very little you are allowed to say at all.[13]

Leo XIII commits himself to the historicity of every statement not obviously a quotation in the Old Testament. That is absolutely and finally hopeless.... It is not that one wants to deny what the Pope has said. On the contrary one has the strongest reasons for wishing to justify them. But on such matters as this, one simply cannot refuse to be convinced by the evidence.... I wish to goodness that the Pope would never speak at all except when he means to define *ex cathedra*. Then we should know where we are.[14]

---

[12] Letter, June 18, 1920, Cambridge University Library [hereafter CUL], Morison Papers, I, 16–18. Letters held by CUL are quoted here by permission of the Syndics of Cambridge University Library.

[13] Letter, October 12, 1911, SEC 20–22–52.

[14] Letter, July 22, 1920, CUL, Morison Papers, I, 16–18.

And speaking of a new archbishop who had asked him to design his new armorial bearings, he recounted:

> It is an amusing story. He would not look at the Heralds' College, on the alleged ground that it is a heretical institution, really because he did not want to pay fees. He thought (*o sancta simplicitas*) that the Pope would confirm some faked arms for nothing. Now he has discovered that the Apostolic palm needs to be greased, just as much as the Herald's College. So he is assuming a coat, that I have made up for his See, without asking authority from anyone.... On the whole, since he will not do the only really honest thing, and get a grant from the Heralds' College, I would just as soon that he simply adopted this by his own Metropolitical authority, as that he went to a central Italian bishop to get it approved.[15]

Clearly Adrian Fortescue was no ultramontanist! His exercise of critical ability (in strictly private correspondence), while remaining thoroughly loyal and obedient; his sense of history; and indeed his sense of humor offer a helpful guide to those participating in any discussion of possible reforms to the papacy.

Throughout *The Early Papacy* Dr. Fortescue refers to the importance of "what the Church teaches today" about the papacy. An appendix containing excerpts from the *Catechism of the Catholic Church* is therefore included, which selects some paragraphs as a guide to the reader on the teaching of the Church about the papacy. They are, however, extracts, and they themselves quote many other pertinent documents. A full understanding of the teaching of the Church about the papacy requires careful study of the

---

[15] Letter, July 26, 1921, CUL, Morison Papers, I, 16–18.

Catechism itself and the documents on which it draws. A list of suggestions for further reading is also appended. To those suggestions should be added the catechetical talks on the office of the Bishop of Rome delivered by our beloved Holy Father Pope Benedict XVI at the Wednesday general audiences early in his pontificate and preeminently his homily on the occasion of his taking possession of his Cathedral of St. John Lateran on May 7, 2005, where he spoke explicitly on the teaching authority and power of the Pope:

> This power of teaching frightens many people in and outside the Church. They wonder whether freedom of conscience is threatened or whether it is a presumption opposed to freedom of thought. It is not like this. The power that Christ conferred upon Peter and his Successors is, in an absolute sense, a mandate to serve. The power of teaching in the Church involves a commitment to the service of obedience to the faith. The Pope is not an absolute monarch whose thoughts and desires are law. On the contrary: the Pope's ministry is a guarantee of obedience to Christ and to his Word. He must not proclaim his own ideas, but rather constantly bind himself and the Church to obedience to God's Word, in the face of every attempt to adapt it or water it down, and every form of opportunism.[16]

Fortescue's other writings on some of the subjects raised in the following pages may be of interest. They include his book *The Greek Fathers* (1908)[17]; his paper "The Eastern Schism", published in W. H. Cologan's *Folia Fugitiva* (1907); his CTS pamphlets *Pope Gregory VII* (1909), *The Branch Theory*

---

[16] *L'Osservatore Romano*, no. 19 (May 11, 2005), p. 3.

[17] Recently reissued as *The Greek Fathers: Their Lives and Writings* (San Francisco: Ignatius Press, 2007).

(1910), *Rome and Constantinople* (1910), and *Catholic Because Roman Catholic* (1917); and his book *Donatism* (1917).

I am grateful to all those who have assisted with this edition. It is my hope that the further republication of these essays by Ignatius Press, edited so that they can be read without difficulty today, will contribute in a small way to a *ressourcement* with regard to the office of the papacy among those in communion with the Bishop of Rome and that it will assist those outside this communion to seek it out, confident that it is willed by Christ for all who would be joined to him in this life and in the next.

Alcuin Reid
February 22, 2008

NOTE
TO THE READER
FROM THE ORIGINAL EDITION

These chapters were first published in the *Tablet*, from September 6 to November 8, 1919, in answer to a challenge to prove the papal claims by documents of the early Church, not later than the Synod of Chalcedon in 451. They are reprinted and revised, by permission of the editor, in the hope that a collection of texts from that period may be of use to Catholics. All are translated into English, and references are given throughout.

Of course, the limit of the year 451 is an absolutely arbitrary one, accepted only because the opponent chose it. No period of any kind ends with the Synod of Chalcedon. The early Church would best be brought down to the peace of Constantine in 312, the ancient world perhaps (though rather arbitrarily) to the deposition of Romulus Augustulus in 476. The next end of a period, in Church history, would be the beginning of the great Eastern schism (intrusion of Photius in 858). But any fixing of periods in history is only a matter of convenience for classifying. Church history, like any other, is one continuous story throughout.

Adrian Fortescue

Letchworth, Septuagesima, 1920

I

The Appeal to Antiquity

Quite a number of Christians of all denominations now
discuss the possibility of healing, at last, the schisms that are
the tragedy and the scandal of Christendom. It seems that
the war of 1914–1918 had something to do with the spread
of this feeling. The war in no way really affected the question. The scandal of our unhappy divisions was just as great
before 1914. Yet it must count as some good out of so much
evil if the soldiers, perhaps especially the army chaplains
who returned, became more conscious of it. They saw in
the Allied armies groups of men, all professing to follow
the same Master, yet, even in the face of death, unable to
say their prayers together.

Much of this discussion concerns a possible amalga-
mation of Protestant bodies. So far it does not affect Catholics; except that we can, we must, sympathize with any
attempt to heal any schism, at least in the hope that such
movements may lead eventually to the reunion that alone
really matters.

From whichever camp a man approaches the question of reunion, he must see that no reconciliation can be anything like adequate unless it involves that communion, by far the largest of all, which obeys the Pope of Rome. One party in the Church of England is specially conscious of this: the Romanizing section of the High Church group. In this section there are men, clergymen, but laymen too, who have come around in an astonishing way from the ideas of the Reformers. They not only long for reunion with the Holy See; they are prepared to accept the Pope's primacy, to accept it, within limits, as being of divine right.

But there is papacy and papacy. In earlier days, they urge, the papacy was not what it has become in the Roman communion since. In the early Church the papacy was a far more moderate authority; there was a primacy then, but it was a constitutional primacy. Out of this, in the Roman communion, an unconstitutional papacy, an irresponsible autocracy, has grown. The Anglican of this school could submit to a constitutional papacy, not to the arbitrary rule now claimed by the Pope. So, such Anglicans suggest, let us concentrate on the question of the papacy in the early Church. In order to determine a limit, let us take the year of the Synod of Chalcedon, 451, and discuss what the Church recognized as the Pope's authority before that. The advantage of such a limit is that (in this view) all branches of the Church—Roman Catholics, Orthodox and Anglicans—acknowledge the Church at least down to that year; to all of us this early period is the standard, and we all claim that our religion is that of the Catholic Church at least down to 451. The Bible, then, and the voice of the Church down to 451 supply a common ground for discussion. The Romanizing Anglican is confident that by examining this standard period, we shall find that there was then indeed an acknowledged Roman primacy (so far he is on our side, against many of his co-religionists) but that it was a constitutional primacy. Therefore Romanists, too, accepting this undoubted standard, will see themselves obliged, not indeed to give up the papacy, but to reduce it to its primitive limits. When they do so, the great hindrance to reunion between them and the rest of the Church will be happily removed. The severed Church will heal her gaping wounds, the present scandal of Christendom will cease, the seamless robe of Christ will again be united, under a constitutional primate. Each side in our long controversy will have yielded something— they, their rejection of any primacy; we, our arbitrary monarchy—so we shall meet halfway. Meanwhile, it has been urged, we have already in this original constitutional papacy the authority of the Church that an Anglican can recognize and obey. It is no use to say that the constitutional papacy no longer exists, on his own showing. It lives in its voices in the documents of that early age still extant; it is a living authority, just as much as the Bible. Obey what that primitive papacy commanded in like circumstances, what you think it would command today, if it had not disappeared under the exaggerations of a later age; and you have your authority for the Church, at least as good an authority as that of the Protestant, who obeys what the Bible commands in similar circumstances.

Such a position is riddled with impossibilities. First, we cannot admit that it is necessary for a Catholic today to examine the documents of the years 1 to 451 in order to know what is the nature of the primacy that Christ gave to his Church. We believe in a Church that exists and lives all days, even to the end of the world, guided by Christ, infallible in faith and morals as long as she exists. We have exactly the same confidence in the divine guidance of the Church in 1870 as in 451. To be obliged to hark back some fifteen hundred years, to judge for yourself, according to the measure of your scholarship, what the documents of that period imply, would be the end of any confidence in a living authority. It is a far worse criterion for religion than the old Protestant idea of the Bible only. We say that it is impossible for a plain man to make up his own religion out of sixty-six books (seventy-three if you count the deuterocanonical books), written at different times, and not specially for his difficulties now. It is even more obviously impossible if to these you add about a hundred volumes of Migne.[1] All these methods of taking some early documents, whether the Bible or the Fathers, and making them your standard, mean simply a riot of private judgment on each point of religion. People disagree and will continue to disagree about the interpretation of ancient documents, of early Fathers, even more than of the books in the Bible. When one Anglican has admitted that he finds a constitutional papacy in the Fathers and councils down to 451, another Anglican, possibly still more learned in patrology, will deny that these old texts mean any real primacy at all. We shall go on arguing about the meaning of the Fathers even more hopelessly than we have argued for centuries about the meaning of Matthew 16:18, when Jesus said to Peter, "Thou art Peter; and upon this rock I will build my church, and the gates of hell shall not prevail against it" (Douay-Rheims). The only possible real standard is a living authority, an authority alive in the world at this moment, that can answer your difficulties, reject

---

[1] *Patrologiæ cursus completus: Series græca*, 161 vols. (Paris, 1886); *Series latina*, 221 vols. (Paris, 1844–1866): the great collection of the works of the Greek and Latin Fathers, edited by Fr. J. P. Migne.

a false theory as it arises and say who is right in disputed interpretations of ancient documents.[2]

A further fallacy of this view is that, because Romanists, Orthodox and Anglicans (not really all Anglicans, by the way; the Evangelicals acknowledge the Bible only and have Article VI plainly in their favor) recognize the Church down to 451, this is therefore to be the standard. This is the usual High Church fallacy of supposing that these communions together make up the Church, and then taking as your standard the points on which they agree. The Armenian and Copt, both representing large national churches, both baptized and not having (in some sense) lost their baptismal life, object very strongly to including the Synod of Chalcedon. They want

---

[2] The Rev. F. W. Puller, as one instance, makes much of appeal to antiquity as the one criterion of the true faith and dismisses any other attitude as "rationalistic, not to say heretical". (*The Primitive Saints and the See of Rome*, 3rd ed. [London: Longmans, 1914], author's preface, pp. xxviii–xxix, and appendix M, pp. 432–33.)

Our objection to antiquity as the final standard is not that we admit or fear that antiquity may be against the claims of the Pope. On the contrary, we are convinced it supports them entirely as the quotations in this book, I hope, will show. Our objection is that antiquity as the final standard throws every article of faith to each man's private opinion, just as hopelessly as appeal to the Bible only. Good and learned men of different sects disagree as to what the early Fathers believed, what exactly their words mean, as much as they disagree about the teaching of the Bible. The Anglican appeals to antiquity against the Pope; the Presbyterian appeals to the same antiquity against any bishops; the Unitarian and nearly all Protestant leaders in Germany and Holland now appeal against the Trinity. The appeal to the faith of the early Church means really what you, by virtue of your studies, think the early Church believed. This is as essentially Protestant, as subjective, as to make each man's private judgment of the meaning of Bible texts his final standard; and it is fifty times as difficult in practice. The Catholic criterion is what the living Church, guided always by God, teaches today. This, and this alone, is a real, objective standard of belief, about which there neither is nor can be any doubt, once you know what the Church of Christ is.

to stop at 431. But then the Assyrian[3] could object to this equally strongly, quite as strongly as the Anglican objects to the First Vatican Council. The Arian, if such a thing is left, objects to Nicea in 325. So you will have to come back to the Bible only. Then we shall quarrel over the question concerning which books form the Bible; and the higher critic, the Broad Anglican, will by no means admit that all that is in even the protocanonical books is authentic. Where is your standard now? What is the good of a standard that already supposes what you are going to prove?

Further, the idea of a dead past in which the Church was united, and a present in which it is not, means really that the original Church, founded by Christ, has ceased to exist. A society that has become three or more separate societies no longer exists. This is so obvious that no one would think of disputing it, unless he had some controversial axe to grind. Consider the case of any other society, where no one has anything at stake in his view of what happened. In 1914 there was an Austro-Hungarian State. Now, that state broke up into a German-Austrian Republic, a separated Hungary, a Czecho-Slovak Republic, part of Poland, a kingdom of Southern Slavs. What was the result? Where is the original Austro-Hungarian State? It no longer exists.

We cannot then admit any criterion of this kind, nor any necessity to go back to some ancient period, and documents of a former age, to find in them the authority of the Church of Christ. That would not be a living authority at all. In the same way a man could pretend that he belongs to the Church of Jupiter and that he finds in the works of

---

[3] The Assyrian Church of the East, once popularly known as the Nestorian Church, which rejected the Council of Ephesus, 431.

Livy the authority that governs his church. But who would admit that there is such a church now existing or that these are a living authority?

Our view of the Church is altogether different. We believe that, whatever may happen, the Church of Christ still lives and will live to the end of the world. Christ said so. She remains always what he founded—one united society. Her rebel children may leave her and set up rival churches of their own. This is tragic; it is the great tragedy of Christendom; but it does not affect the unity of the original Church, for unity is of her essence. Nothing can destroy that, because her Founder is almighty and promised that she should last always, till the end of the world. The fact that many Christians have left the Church of Christ is not new; it is almost as old as Christianity itself. From the time of the first Gnostic sects, of which we read in the New Testament, through the great Arian schism, through Nestorianism and Monophysitism, through the Paulicians and the schism of Cerularius, through the heresies of the Albigensians and the Reformation, there has been a procession of sects cut away from the Church that Christ founded. Anglicans are fond of saying that it is a "fact" that the Catholic Church is now divided. It is a fact that there are many Christians who have left her, that Christendom is divided; it is not a fact that the Church is divided. They might as well say that it is a fact that the Church was no longer visibly one in Arian days. If ever it were so, then the original Church would no longer exist; the gates of hell would have prevailed. Many things are possible, heresy and schism are possible; but that is not possible. So we believe in the one visible Church today just as much as that there was such a Church from Pentecost to the year 451. We look to this Church for guidance in religion, as she is now, as she teaches this year. The volumes of Migne are of great interest, but they are not necessary for us to know what the Church of Christ teaches. There is, indeed, a special halo around the venerable antiquity of the first centuries; but the Church was not more guided by our Lord then than she is now. The criterion of faith about the papacy for us is what the Catholic Church teaches today. We shall never get forward in discussion with people on any one dogma till we agree about this: that the authority of the Church today is the criterion for all dogmas.

But this does not mean that we refuse to discuss early texts about the papacy. On the contrary, we are always doing so, and we claim that these early texts confirm what the Church teaches today. The position is this: there are two kinds of proof for any dogma. The main proof, the most efficient in every way, the proof that is the real motive for every Catholic, is simply that this dogma is taught now by the Church of Christ, that Christ has given to his Church his own authority, so that we can trust the Church as we trust Christ himself. "Who heareth you, heareth me" (Lk 10:16). The argument is the same for every dogma (that is why the Catholic position is essentially simple, in spite of apparent complexity); it can be understood by the most ignorant, as the religion of Christ must be (it is impossible for every child and peasant to make up his own Christianity for himself by his interpretation of Scripture or the Fathers down to 451). This position admits no vagaries of private judgment for each dogma. No variety of interpretation is possible as to what the Catholic Church of today teaches, or, if such misunderstanding should occur, the Church is there to declare her mind. Even the most fundamental dogmas rest ultimately on the teaching of the Catholic Church today, even, for instance, that of the Holy Trinity. All we suppose, before we come to the Church, is that our Lord Jesus Christ was a man sent by God and whom we must follow if we wish to serve God in the proper way; that he founded one visible Church, to which his followers should belong; that this Church is, as a matter of historic fact, the communion of Rome (not, however, supposing anything about the papacy, but supposing only visible unity and historic continuity). This much must be presupposed and therefore does not rest on the authority of the Church. All else does.

But there is also another kind of argument for each dogma, taking each separately and proving that this was taught by Christ and has been believed from the beginning. This line of argument is neither so convincing nor so safe. It does now involve our private judgment as to whether the ancient texts do, or do not, really prove what we claim. It requires knowledge of the texts, of dead languages; to be efficient it requires considerable scholarship. It is impossible that our Lord should give us a religion requiring all this before you know what it is. This direct proof of each dogma can be only confirmation of the general argument for all, taken from the present teaching of the Church. But it is a most valuable confirmation, which we are always ready to offer, as long as it is understood that it is not the main reason of our belief. I am quite sure that Matthew 16:18 and the Church Fathers Clement of Rome, Irenaeus, Chrysostom and Augustine all say what I believe about the Bishop of Rome. But I do not base my faith on what they say; I do not really care a jot whether *convenire ad* means "agree with" or "go to". I base my faith on what the Catholic Church of today says. That alone is quite enough for all of us; in this we have an argument perfectly clear, convincing, final, the same for the student of patrology as for a peasant who can neither read nor write.

Nor can we admit the right of opponents to fix a period of history, challenging us to prove some particular dogma from texts taken from that period only. Suppose a man said that what inspires him with confidence is the Church between the years 250 and 300; would we kindly prove that matrimony is a sacrament, by documents from that period only? We must not forget that the Fathers did not write their letters or preach their sermons with a view to supplying evidences of the faith of their time for future controversialists. It is often a matter of chance (unless we say it is Providence) whether some particular early writer does, or does not, happen to mention a certain point of his faith. Even the New Testament does not profess to be an ordered textbook of dogmatic theology; it consists of four accounts of the life of Christ, an incomplete account of what the apostles were doing for a few years, some letters and a mysterious prophecy. The argument from silence is of little value in the case of such documents. When the Fathers of Chalcedon met, they were out to explain their faith about the natures of Christ, not about the rights of the Roman Patriarch.

Yet it so happens that we have exceptionally clear documents about the papacy from the first four and a half centuries. Certainly we can prove all that is now of the faith concerning the Pope by texts chosen from that period. Only this had to be said first, because we cannot concede that such a test is the final one or that people have the right to fix dates and challenge us to prove our dogma from between those dates only. This would be the right course if Christ had said: "Go and teach all nations, until Photius is intruded at Constantinople; and I am with you all days, even to the year 451."

The Constitutional Papacy

Before we examine what the documents before 451 say about the position of the Bishop of Rome, there are several points that we must consider. First of all, there is a distinction, too often forgotten. If it could be proved that the early Church believed, as part of her faith, the contrary of what we believe now, or anything logically incompatible with our belief, this would be exceedingly serious; it would, indeed, be the refutation of our position, since we maintain that the faith does not change. But it is not at all the same thing, even if it were true, to say that we could not prove that the early Church did believe what we believe now. Suppose, for the sake of argument, that we could find no statement of any kind about some dogma; this would not affect our position. There would then be no proof, either for or against the dogma, in the given period. We should believe it all the same, because of a definition made at another time. It is not only the Church of the first four and a half centuries that is guided by the Holy Spirit. There is no proof of the Trinity in the epistle of St. James. As a matter of fact, this

is not the case here. We have all the evidence we can require
that the Catholic Church in the first four and a half centuries did believe what we believe about the papacy. The
point is mentioned only because people so often confuse
not saying a thing is true with saying that it is not true.

We have, then, to show that the early Church recognized the papacy. But before we do so, we must have a
clear idea of what the papacy is. Shall we say that there was
a constitutional primacy in the early Church but not the
unconstitutional primacy now claimed by the Pope? This
distinction is futile. It is one more case of the way in which
people who have never been trained to think accurately are
content with a form of words, having no definite idea behind
it. In the same way, there are folk who will tell you that
they do believe in a Real Presence in the Eucharist, but in
a spiritual presence; the Church of Rome, however, teaches
a material presence. If only they would get behind words
to ideas, they would understand that what we need is a
definition of "spiritual presence". What do they mean by
the spiritual presence of a body? Then, perhaps, when they
have thought a little about that, they will find that what
they mean is what the Church of Rome means, only
expressed by a careless phrase—just so with this expression:
"constitutional" and "unconstitutional" papacy. What do you
mean by "constitutional papacy"? You must first define that;
then we shall be able to say whether it does or does not
satisfy what the Catholic Church teaches on the subject.

As a matter of fact, there is a sense in which the papacy,
as it is claimed by Catholics today, must be called constitutional, and a sense in which it is not so. If by constitutional papacy you mean a primate who reigns but does not
govern, merely the first among equals, a primate who has
no real jurisdiction beyond that of any other bishop but

only a primacy of honor, only the right to sign first among others, then certainly we demand more than this for the Pope. Yet we should not admit that the Pope's authority is unconstitutional either. Is the authority of the commander-in-chief of an army at war constitutional or unconstitutional? Do we consider that he has no authority beyond the right to march in front of the army, to go about among the soldiers, exhorting them to be brave, or, since undoubtedly he claims real authority, the right to settle the plan of campaign, to give orders that all the army must obey, shall we on this account describe his rights as unconstitutional?

Of course, the authority of the Pope is constitutional, as it always has been. The Pope is not an irresponsible tyrant who can do anything with the Church that he likes. He is bound on every side by the constitution of the Church. Someday a Catholic theologian ought to write a treatise on the limitations of the papacy.[1] This would do much good among Protestants, who are accustomed to think of us as putting the whole system of our religion at the mercy of one man, and of such a man as Rodrigo Borgia.[2] The Pope's authority, in the first place, is limited to matters of *religion*, that is, of faith and morals and such things as canon law, liturgy, marriage cases, ecclesiastical censures and so on, which are part of faith and morals. The Pope has no authority from Christ in temporal matters, in questions of politics[3]

---

[1] In 1987 Patrick Granfield published *The Limits of the Papacy* (London and New York: Darton Longmann and Todd). While this work contains some useful material, it is motivated by a reaction against Pope John Paul II's exercise of papal authority in disciplining dissenting theologians.

[2] Pope Alexander VI (1492–1503): probably the most infamous "bad Pope".

[3] When Popes in the past interfered in politics we must say either that this authority was given to them by the consent of Europe or that in this they exceeded their charter. Dante was as good a Catholic and as great a theologian

(people who kept on badgering that the Pope should say
who was right in the war did not realize this). He has no
authority from Christ to teach mathematics, geography or
history. His authority is ecclesiastical authority; it goes no
further than that of the Church herself. But even in religious matters the Pope is bound, very considerably, by the
divine constitution of the Church. There are any number
of things that the Pope cannot do in religion. He cannot
modify or touch in any way one single point of the revelation Christ gave to the Church; his business is only to
guard this against attack and false interpretation. We believe
that God will so guide him that his decisions of this nature
will be nothing more than a defense or unfolding of what
Christ revealed. The Pope can neither make nor unmake a
sacrament; he cannot affect the essence of any sacrament in
any way. He cannot touch the Bible; he can neither take
away a text from the inspired Scriptures nor add one to
them. He has no fresh inspiration or revelation. His business is to believe the revelation of Christ, as all Catholics
believe it, and to defend it against heresy. He cannot take
away the divine authority of any of his fellow bishops as
long as they are Catholic bishops in normal possession of
their sees, though he can, as chief authority of the Church

as ever has been. What he says in his *Monarchy* we may all say (see *Mon.* iii,
cap. 12–16). Theologians sometimes speak of an indirect power of the Church
in temporal matters. There seems no need for this phrase. The Church has
authority in her own sphere (religion) and so, of course, in whatever belongs
to this sphere or is necessary to it. She does not teach history; but some
matters of history are also matters of religion, as, for instance, that Christ
spoke certain words, that Peter was Bishop of Rome. This consideration will
cover all cases of indirect power in temporal things. It is true that sometimes
ecclesiastical authorities, as others, have suffered from a tendency to enlarge
their boundaries.

on earth, under certain circumstances try, suspend or depose an unworthy bishop.

The Pope can, in extraordinary circumstances, rearrange dioceses;[4] he cannot abolish the universal episcopate. The Church of Christ, by her Founder's constitution, is ruled by bishops who are the successors of the apostles, among whom, as among the apostles, one of their number is chief. Each Catholic bishop receives his jurisdiction from God, though he must use it in the union of his fellow bishops and in canonical obedience to the Bishop of Rome, who is his chief. The Pope is not, in the absolute sense, head of the Church; the head of the Church is Jesus Christ, our Lord, as our English catechism says. The Pope is the vicar of that head and is therefore the visible head of the Church on earth, having authority delegated from Christ over the Church on earth only, just as every diocesan bishop has authority delegated from Christ over his diocese only. If the Pope is a monarch, he is a very constitutional monarch indeed, bound on all sides by the constitution of the Church, as this has been given her by Christ. The chief difference between the Pope and his fellow Catholics is not the picturesque ceremonial attached to his office; it is not that compelling attraction of the white-robed Pontiff in the Vatican and all the rest of it, which so impresses Mr. N. P. Williams.[5] It is the awful responsibility he bears before his Master: to maintain the traditional faith unaltered, to discharge

---

[4] The extreme case of this in Church history is the concordat between Pius VII and Napoleon in 1801. Extreme measures were then demanded, after the utter upheaval of the Revolution and the schism of the constitutional clergy. In 1801 eighty-one of the old bishops were still alive—forty-five resigned their sees; thirty-six did not resign. But others did so later, and many soon died. In 1818 only four anticoncordat bishops were left.

[5] *Our Case as against Rome* (London: Longmans, 1918), p. 91.

loyally the stewardship of which he will have to give a stern account, to set a good example to his brother bishops. Because of this responsibility, he deserves the sympathy of us, on whom God has not laid so heavy a burden; he needs the prayers of his brethren more than any man on earth.

The question has been raised whether the other bishops are to consider themselves brothers or sons of the Pope. The question is vain; there is a sense in which all Catholics are brothers, another sense in which all bishops are brothers, another again in which the bishop is father of his flock, and the Pope is father of all Christians. Obviously, in addressing a superior we use a humbler title for ourselves; and he, by the same rule of courtesy, uses the humbler one for himself. We think of our bishop as our father in God and call him so; he addresses us as "dear brethren in Jesus Christ". Nuns call their abbess "mother"; she calls each one of them "sister". So other bishops address the Pope as "Holy Father", and he calls them "venerable brethren". Both titles are right; it depends on which basis of relationship you consider. The Pope is the spiritual father of all Christians, including his fellow bishops; yet the episcopate is one—all bishops are equal and brothers, as bishops, so the Pope always calls them "brethren".[6] Our Lord himself is both the firstborn among many brethren and father of the world to come.

Now, leaving aside all verbal disputes as to whether we are to call the Pope constitutional or unconstitutional, let us see what his authority really is, as defined by the Catholic Church today. We shall then be able to show that it

---

[6] Customarily he addressed every cardinal as "son", because a cardinal is, in principle, either a regionary deacon, a parish priest of the Roman diocese, or a suburban bishop of the province. So he has a special filial relation to the Roman Metropolitan.

was the same in the first four and a half centuries. When a man understands this, he may call it anything he likes.

Has the papacy grown? In a sense it has, just as every dogma of the Church may be said to have grown. We come here to that question of the development of doctrine, of which much might be said. At any rate, let us understand clearly that there is no special question of the papacy here. If you say that the papacy has grown, you must equally say that the doctrine of the Real Presence has grown since the definition of Transubstantiation in 1215, that the doctrine of the Trinity grew by the decision of 325. That is to say, when a point of faith is disputed, when some new heresy arises, the Church makes her mind clear by defining more explicitly what she has always held. She forbids a false interpretation of the faith, and so she makes it more definite. Hence vague statements, harmless before controversy began, become impossible after the definition. But we do not admit that this development means any real addition to the faith; it is only a more explicit assertion of the old faith, necessary in view of false interpretations. A conspicuous case of this is the declaration of papal infallibility by the First Vatican Council. The early Church recognized that the Pope has the final word in matters of faith, no less than in those of discipline, that she herself is protected by God against heresy. Put that together, and you have, implicitly, what the Council defined.

Besides this there has been real growth in the *use* of the Pope's authority. Many matters, such as canonization of saints, approval of religious orders and so on, once settled by the bishop of the diocese, now go to Rome. Appeals are far more frequent and about smaller matters. Patriarchal and metropolitan authority over bishops has diminished very much. There has been a constant process of centralizing.

This was caused in various ways. Increased facilities of communication with headquarters had something to do with it. At one time, to appeal to Rome meant a serious journey for the bearer of a letter; now it costs but a few pennies. Then there is the natural tendency of any society toward centralization. We can observe this almost everywhere. It becomes so much easier, shorter; it saves so much trouble to go straight to headquarters at once. Then you have the decision of the supreme authority, and no possibility of further dispute. Such cases become precedents for next time. Again, the Protestant revolt of the sixteenth century had its natural result in increased centralization among those who remained faithful. A reaction of greater loyalty, at any rate of greater manifestation of loyalty to authority, is inevitable among those who abhor the rebellion. The spectacle of the anarchy of Protestantism, a spectacle offered to us more plainly each century, has its effect on Catholics. That is what comes of "No Popery". What Catholic, seeing the state of the Church of England today, does not thank God that he has given to us an authority to settle disputes of religion? Lastly, the Reformation drew away from the Church possible centrifugal elements. But all this is only a development of canon law in details, about the opportuneness of which each man may form his own opinion. We take the Church as she is, because she is the Church of Christ; and we know that Christ will not allow her to lead us astray in anything essential. Consider a parallel case in the state. In the process of time it will often happen that the administration of certain departments concerning roads, postal services and railways is taken over from municipal authority by the central government. This is a matter of arrangement and convenience. You may think such changes an advantage, or you may prefer the power of the municipalities. In any case, you have to take the arrangements as they are; nor does this affect your loyalty to your country. What we claim then is not that there has been no modification of canon law in the government of the Church, in the relations of the ordinary, the metropolitan and the Pope. Our position is that nothing essential is altered by such modification. The essence of the papacy today is what it has always been. What we hold *de fide*[7] about the Bishop of Rome is what the Catholic Church has held, the belief on which she has acted, always. It remains to see exactly what is our faith on this point.

---

[7] *De fide definita*, that is, defined as a dogma of the Catholic faith and hence requiring the assent of faith; see L. Ott, *Fundamentals of Catholic Dogma* (Rockford, Ill.: Tan Books, 1974), p. 8.

3

What Are the Papal Claims?

It is now time to say what the papacy does involve. Before quoting texts to prove it, we must state the thesis to be proved. Leaving aside vague and useless distinctions, such as that between a supposed "constitutional" and a supposed "unconstitutional" primacy, let us draw up a direct statement of what the Catholic Church today claims concerning the position of the Pope. It will then be our business to prove this from documents written not later than the year 451.

What we believe about the rights of the Pope is contained in these four points: (1) The Pope is the chief bishop, primate and leader of the whole Church of Christ on earth. (2) He has episcopal jurisdiction over all members of the Church. (3) To be a member of the Catholic Church, a man must be in communion with the Pope. (4) The providential guidance of God will see to it that the Pope shall never commit the Church to error in any matter of religion.

There are further details concerning the Pope's position. To make a complete statement of all his rights and duties would require a long treatise of canon law. But these further

details are mostly consequences of the four principles we
have drawn up. Others are matters of canon law, arranged
by consent of the Church, for which we do not claim divine
right. We submit that our four points are an adequate statement of the essence of the papacy. If a man concedes these,
he will satisfy what is required of a Catholic *de fide*. Each
now requires some explanation:

1. *The Pope is the chief bishop, primate and leader of the whole
Church of Christ on earth.* This is the first, the least claim.
To a great extent it is admitted by most High Church Anglicans, at least in the sense that the Bishop of Rome is the
first bishop of Christendom. The Eastern churches, not in
communion with us, admit this much too. No one com-
petent to discuss the question would place any other bishop
over the Pope, as being a greater authority than he is. Still
less would any respectable theologian (of any persuasion)
now count a temporal prince as having jurisdiction in Church
matters, certainly not as having ecclesiastical jurisdiction over
the Pope. Moreover, this first point, most evident of all in
antiquity, is contained a fortiori in those that follow, so that
it will hardly be worthwhile to quote many texts here. What
it comes to in practice is this: the Bishop of Rome is the
right person to take the lead in any common action of the
whole Church; particularly it is his right to summon a general council, to preside at it, either himself or by his legate,
and to confirm its decisions. But this does not mean that
he has always done each of these things. To say that a man
has a right does not mean that he has always used his right.
There have been councils, afterward recognized as ecumenical, that were not summoned by the Pope. Our point of
view, in this case, is that the Pope should have been summoned, if the council were intended to be ecumenical; but
then the Pope accepted what had happened and by so doing

made up all irregularity in the summons. Nor did the Pope preside at every meeting now counted among the general councils, not even by his legate. Here again we have the same case. It is the Pope's right to preside, if the council is ecumenical. This, at least, will be admitted by most of those who concede much less than we claim for him. In an ecclesiastical council it seems obvious that a bishop should preside. What other bishop can anyone suggest but the first bishop of the Church? So again, if the Pope did not preside, this shows only that in this matter, too, the proper course was not taken. There are two notable instances in which the Pope had nothing to do with either the summoning or the holding of a general council; they are the second council, in 381, and the fifth, in 553, both held at Constantinople. We come to a radical question: What is the real test of an ecumenical council? Synods have been held in all sorts of circumstances, by all sorts of bishops. Some of these we recognize as general councils of the whole Church.[1] Why? The test cannot be the number of bishops who met or the representative places from which they came. The synod of 381 was summoned by Emperor Theodosius; he had no idea that he was calling together a general council; his object was to settle a dispute about the lawful bishop of Constantinople, a purely local matter. Only about 150 bishops attended, all from Eastern sees. The West was not represented at all. In what sense can this be called ecumenical? Again, in 553 only 160 bishops signed the acts; except for eight Africans, all were from the East. This council was summoned by Emperor Justinian I. The only way to explain these councils, from any point of view, is that they were

---

[1] "General" council and "ecumenical" council mean the same thing, i.e., a universal council of bishops binding upon the universal Church.

ecumenical neither in their summons nor in their sessions. If they are now counted as such, they owe this solely to the later ratification of the Church (as far as the Church did ratify them). Acceptance by the whole Church, then, becomes the final test of ecumenicity for a synod. It can supplement whatever was lacking before. This brings us to the Pope's third right regarding general councils: he ratifies them. Without this, none are ecumenical; the Pope's ratification can make up for any defect in the holding of the synod. The obvious parallel is the act by which a king can ratify anything done by Parliament without his consent hitherto, as Charles II did (to some extent) in 1660. Again it is difficult to see what objection an Anglican could make to the requirement of papal ratification of general councils. He, too, needs the consent of the whole Church, if a council is to be considered ecumenical. But the consent of the whole Church must include that of the chief bishop; where is the consent of all, if the first patriarch does not agree? The difference here is that we attach more importance to the consent of the Pope than would the Anglican. But, so far, we can all agree that no council is general unless the Pope agrees to it.

2. *The Pope has episcopal jurisdiction over all members of the Church.* This is what the First Vatican Council declares, that the Pope has "immediate power of jurisdiction, which is really episcopal", over people of every rite and rank in the Church.[2] It is not, so far, our object to prove any of these principles; first we want to establish what the Catholic thesis is. The statement that the Pope has episcopal jurisdiction over the whole Church is short and easy to remember.

---

[2] Conc. Vat. I, Denzinger-Schönmetzer [hereafter DS], *Enchiridion symbolorum*, 36th ed. (St. Louis: Herder, 1976), no. 3060.

But, as generally happens, it loses in completeness what it gains in brevity. By the very fact that it is universal, over the diocesan bishop himself, papal jurisdiction is greater than that of any one local bishop. It is summed up by the Fathers of Vatican I as "full power to feed, rule and govern" the Church,[3] by which they repeat the declaration of the Council of Florence in 1439.[4] For a general statement, it is sufficiently accurate to say that what authority a bishop has over his flock, the Pope has over the whole Church. Like the jurisdiction of the local bishop, that of the Pope, by divine institution, extends only to matters of religion; as the local bishop is monarch of his diocese, so is the Pope monarch of the whole Church on earth; as the bishop is vicar of Christ, representing to his flock the authority of Christ in all religious matters, so is the Pope the supreme vicar of Christ to all the faithful on earth. Both Florence and Vatican I are careful to state that this supreme jurisdiction of the Pope is not meant in any way to diminish the divine right by which each bishop rules his own flock—placed by the Holy Spirit over his see, as real pastor and successor of the apostles. Papal authority is to "assert, strengthen and defend" the authority of other bishops.[5] There is a consideration that may help people to realize that the authority of the Pope is not the great exception to the normal order of Church government that they sometimes think. Anglicans often tell us that all bishops are equal, as if this principle were an objection to the papacy. So they are, as

---

[3] DS 3059.

[4] DS 1307.

[5] Conc. Vat. I, DS 3061; cf. Council of Florence: *Lætentur*, "salvis videlicet privilegiis omnibus et iuribus eorum" (all their rights and privileges remaining intact), DS 1308.

far as the order of the episcopate is concerned. There is only one order of bishops; no one can be, in any sense, more a bishop than another. If a man is ordained Bishop of Rome, he receives exactly the same sacrament as one who is ordained bishop of the smallest suffragan see in the most remote land. The Bishop of Rome, as far as order goes, is no more a bishop than the bishop of Krishnagar.[6] But all bishops are not equal, in the sense that none has authority over any other. In this sense the statement is false and can be proved to be false from the very beginning of Church history. It can be proved false by other examples than that of Rome. From the beginning there have been cases of bishops who had extradiocesan authority, that is, jurisdiction, real jurisdiction, over their fellow bishops. To this day the Anglican must be familiar with the idea of an archbishop, who has authority outside his own diocese over other bishops, though these do not thereby cease to be real ordinaries and do not become merely his auxiliaries. Over archbishops there were still, in some cases, primates, sometimes over primates such great people as exarchs. It is true that most of this extradiocesan jurisdiction has worn thin, in modern times, in the Catholic Church. In the first six centuries it was a very solid authority. Over archbishops, primates, and exarchs stand those greatest bishops of all: the five patriarchs. Their authority was always, is still, very great indeed. It is seen only in the East, because there is but one patriarch in the West,[7]

---

[6] [West Bengal, India.] I beg that prelate's pardon, if ever he were to see this. I took the name of his see by chance out of the *Gerarchia*, as being, to us, an odd-looking one and little known. But there can be no real disrespect in saying that he is as good a bishop as his great brother at Rome.

[7] The so-called minor patriarchates (of Venice and Lisbon, among others) are merely honorary titles.

who is the Pope himself.[8] But the principle is there; it should help anyone who has difficulties to understand at least the possibility of the Pope's jurisdiction over other bishops. The point that seems to make all the difference in appreciating the Pope's position is that this is not an isolated fact. The papacy is the topmost point of a regularly graduated hierarchy of bishops, in which each has authority over those under him. Let us say, as a rough general idea, that, as the archbishop has jurisdiction over his suffragans, as the patriarch has jurisdiction over the ordinaries of his patriarchate, so the chief patriarch has jurisdiction over his brother patriarchs, and so over all Catholics. The parallel is not exact; for it is generally, no doubt rightly, said that other cases of jurisdiction over bishops are only of ecclesiastical institution, whereas we certainly maintain that the papacy was founded by our Lord. Yet it will serve as an illustration and as an answer to what most opponents of the papacy urge. Is it a usurpation of Christ's unique sovereignty that the Pope claims jurisdiction over the whole Church? No more than that every bishop claims monarchical authority over his diocese. Or is there something specially impossible in the idea of a man having authority over other bishops, successors of the apostles as he is himself? Then how about the jurisdiction of an archbishop,

---

[8] In 2006 Pope Benedict XVI relinquished the title "Patriarch of the West" as obsolete in order better to reflect historical and theological reality. The title was introduced in the East, in the ambit of the imperial ecclesiastical system of Justinian (527–565), alongside the four Eastern patriarchates: Constantinople, Alexandria, Antioch and Jerusalem. The Fourth Council of Constantinople (869–870), the Fourth Lateran Council (1215) and the Council of Florence (1439) all listed the Pope as the first of the then five Patriarchs without using the title. It was used in the year 642 by Pope Theodore I, appearing only occasionally thereafter but with no clear meaning. It flourished in the 16th and 17th centuries in the context of a general increase in the Pope's titles, appearing for the first time in the *Annuario Pontificio* in 1863.

a primate or a patriarch? "But Christ is the head of the Church" (cf. Col 1:18). Of course he is. He is the head of each diocese, too, the head of each province and patriarchate. If he can have a visible vicar to represent his authority over the diocese and patriarchate, what difficulty is there against the idea of a still higher vicar of Christ, representing his authority over all? We know that Christ governs, teaches and sanctifies his Church through men, his vicars. Christ baptizes; Christ consecrates; Christ forgives sins; he rules the diocese. Christ rules the whole body, too, at headquarters; here, too, he does so through his minister.

3. *To be a member of the Catholic Church, a man must be in communion with the Pope.* This follows from the Pope's universal jurisdiction. It is the one point that the most advanced Anglican cannot concede. It follows also, and more fundamentally, from the visible unity of the Church; this, once more, is the root of all difference between us and Anglicans (not the papacy at all). If the Church is one united, visible society, all Catholics must be in communion with one another. The Pope is certainly a Catholic, so all must be in communion with him. As a matter of fact, it is not necessary to suppose the Pope, or anything about the papacy, for this point. We could take as our test communion with any man admitted to be a Catholic. No one is a Catholic who is not in communion with every Catholic bishop, with every Catholic curate or with the first poor Irishwoman you may find saying her prayers in the corner of a London church. However, rightly, inevitably we do always name the Pope as the Catholic with whom everyone must be in communion; first, because it is natural to quote the chief Catholic of all; next, because the Pope's Catholicity is certain, whatever may happen. If you take any other Catholic as the man with whom we must all be in communion, this is all right as

long as he is a Catholic; but he may fall away himself—
where is your standard then? The Pope as supreme teacher
cannot fall away from the Church, if his primacy is of divine
institution, as we believe (this does suppose the primacy).
Communion with the Pope then is the obvious, final and
exhaustive criterion of Catholicity. It works both ways. Everyone in that communion is a member of the Catholic Church
(he may be a bad Catholic, of course), and no one else. Whatever other cause can destroy a man's Catholicity will produce
the effect that he is no longer in communion with the Pope.

4. *Providence will see to it that the Pope shall never commit the
Church to error in a matter of religion.* This is the famous "infallibility" of the First Vatican Council. It is as well to state
again plainly what it does mean. It does not mean any sort
of inspiration given to the Pope. It does not mean that he
will always know or understand more about our religion
than anyone else. A Pope might be quite ignorant and a
very poor theologian. He may make a mistake as a private
theologian; only God will take care that he does not commit the whole Church to it. Papal infallibility is a negative
protection. We are confident that God will not allow a certain thing to happen; that is all. It does not mean that the
Pope will always give the wisest or best decision or that
what he says will always be well advised or opportune. He
may not speak at all; he may preserve a regrettable silence,
just when it would be greatly to the good of the Church if
he did speak. But if he does speak, and if he speaks in such
a way as to commit the Church, then what he says will not
be false. It may be inadequate.[9] When does the Pope so

---

[9] As a matter of fact, any statement about God in human language must
be inadequate. We do not claim that anything defined by the Church is an
adequate statement. It is true as far as it goes, as much of the truth as God

speak as to commit the whole Church? This is what we mean by a decision ex cathedra.[10] The First Vatican Council defined that the Pope's decisions ex cathedra cannot be false. It says nothing about any other kind of papal pronouncement; it explains an "ex cathedra" statement as (1) a definition, (2) of dogma on faith or morals that (3) binding on the whole Church. This leaves the Pope as much power of expressing his opinion on any subject as anyone else, of expressing it as forcibly as he thinks necessary, yet without committing us to any theory of special divine protection for such statements, unless he satisfies these conditions. For instance, suppose someone in the course of conversation were to ask the current Pope whether belief in the Holy Trinity be necessary. No doubt he would say, as we all should, that it is most certainly necessary. Very likely he would say this with great emphasis. Yet no one would think that in saying this he were making a new pronouncement ex cathedra.

Understood so, papal infallibility is so obvious a consequence of the primacy that it would seem hardly worth special definition, were it not that some people about 1870 were not yet clear on the point. Put together three ideas: first, that the Pope is the last court of appeal in matters of faith no less than in those of discipline; second, that the decisions of the final court must be accepted as final; and third, that God cannot allow his whole Church to fall into error—and you have the whole of papal infallibility at once.

---

sees fit to reveal to us in our present state. Now, the First Vatican Council (Sess. IV, cap. 4) carefully equates the Pope's infallibility to that of the Church. The point has more importance than seems generally to be realized.

[10] Ex cathedra: "from the Chair", viz., of Peter, i.e., from the supreme teaching authority of the Pope.

We shall show that all these ideas were held by Catholics before 451.

The dogma of Vatican I is a typical case of what we mean by development, stating explicitly what was held implicitly from the beginning. Or put it like this. If the Pope were to pronounce heresy, refusing his communion to all who did not agree with him, then one of two things would follow. Either the Church would be out of communion with her own primate, or she would be committed to heresy. Either means bankruptcy of the whole Catholic system; so God cannot allow either to happen. God cannot allow it to happen; that is all the First Vatican Council says. There are many things that we are confident God cannot allow to happen. He cannot allow anything that would ruin his Church. He cannot allow all bishops suddenly to die without having ordained a successor, because that would be the end of the priesthood. Here we have another case of something God cannot allow to happen—unless he means to abandon his Church and make Christ's promises vain. How would God prevent a Pope from declaring heresy ex cathedra? That we must leave to God. His Providence is almighty; if he intends a thing not to occur, it will not occur. Suppose God promised that a certain kingdom should never go to war, and suppose its king had the power of making war. Then we should be quite sure that, somehow, God would manage that the king never used this power.

If we keep clear the idea of *protection*, that all infallibility means is that God will not allow a certain thing to happen because it would mean the bankruptcy of his Church, many difficulties disappear. It is not necessary that every Pope should be explicitly conscious of it himself. God will take care that he does not make a shipwreck of the Church, whether he knows this or not. Divine protection against error is possible in the case of any man. For all I know, God's Providence may have determined that some popular preacher shall never make a theological mistake in a sermon. If so, the man will certainly not do it. Then he, too, would be infallible, in the sense of the First Vatican Council. One cannot prove that it is not so, in any case (unless the man does make a mistake). All we could say would be that there is no proof of anything of the kind. There is proof in the case of the Pope, because he is the final court of appeal for a Church that Christ promised shall not fail. We have the general idea that God guides all the authorities of the Church. It is quite possible that Providence will take care that any given bishop shall not teach heresy in a pastoral, because, if he did so, it would be extremely unfortunate and difficult for his flock. But we have no certain guarantee here. The bishop can be set right by his superior. The Pope has no superior, in Church matters, on earth; so God must take care that the Pope does not do such a thing, when he commits the whole Church. But we cannot admit any further conditions of infallibility, beyond the fact that the Pope commits the whole Church to a point of faith or morals. Some people try to soften down the dogma by saying that the Pope is infallible, if and when he has sufficiently consulted expert theologians, so that what he says really is what the whole Church believes. This will not do.[11] There is a radical flaw of logic here. Such an infallibility would be no special protection at all. Any man is right, if and when he agrees with the truth (that is what it comes

---

[11] "Romani pontificis definitiones ex sese, non autem ex consensu ecclesiæ, irreformabiles [sunt]" (The definitions of the Roman Pontiff are irreformable of themselves, and not by the consent of the Church), Conc. Vat. I, DS 3074.

to). The negative statement, that God will not allow a certain thing, is absolute under any conditions. We must say that if, to protect the Pope from error, the consultation of theologians or any other means are necessary, then God will see to it that these means are taken. But the Pope will not define heresy ex cathedra, whatever happens. If you say that a man will not die in a certain year, you do not mean that he will not die if nothing happens to cause his death. You mean that nothing will happen to cause his death.

This, then, is what we mean when we say that the Pope is infallible; this is what we undertake to prove from documents before the year 451. All this depends further on three more theses, into which we cannot enter here. They are (1) that our Lord gave these rights to the apostle St. Peter, (2) that St. Peter must have a successor in them and (3) that his successor is the Bishop of Rome.

To establish these here would take too much space. We must be content to prove our four points directly as set out at the beginning.

4

The Pope as Chief

Before we quote our texts, there is yet a remark to be made. Nearly all these quotations are quite well known already. This does not affect their value. If a text proves a thesis, it does not matter at all whether it is now quoted for the first or the hundredth time. They are well known to our opponents, too. Around some of these texts (for instance, those of Ignatius, and especially of Irenaeus) the battle of the Roman primacy has been fought for centuries. Naturally, people who deny the primacy also have something to say about them. In each case they make what attempt they can to show that the writer does not really admit what we claim, in spite of his words. It is the same situation as with Matthew 16:18. It is impossible, in our limited space, to go into the controversy that rages around many texts we quote. There is a whole literature about the famous passage in St. Irenaeus alone. The case is always the same. We quote words, of which the plain meaning seems to be that their writer believed what we believe, in some point. The opponent then tries to strip his words of this meaning; Catholic writers then have to refute his attempt. All this has been done scores of times in each case. Sometimes Protestants fall back on the idea that, when some early authority addresses the Pope in words that state or imply his primacy, all this is only polite compliment. You can, of course, discount the value of many statements by saying that they are only compliment. Maybe someday we shall be told that what all the Fathers of the First Vatican Council defined was only excessive politeness to Pius IX. The answer is that, in all cases, we must suppose that a sane man, who uses definite expressions, means what he says, unless the contrary can be proved. To polish off a statement with which you do not agree by saying that it is not meant, and leave the matter at that, is a silly proceeding.

There is another general issue here. These early Fathers are witnesses of the belief of their time. Now, the value of evidence increases as it is multiplied. We must take the value, not of one text, but of all put together. Here we have a great number of texts that all make for the same point. The fact that all do make for the same point suggests the rea- · sonable interpretation of each. All can be understood naturally, supposing that their writers believed in the primacy of the Pope. If you do not admit that, you have to find a different, often a most tortuous, interpretation for each. The rule of good reasoning is that one simple cause that accounts equally for all the phenomena is to be supposed the real one, unless it be proved false. Now, there is nothing that can even be reasonably suggested to show that the early Fathers did not believe in the primacy. The three or four cases in which someone resists the Pope's order or complains of his action prove nothing of the kind. They prove either that he thought the Pope ill-advised in this particular case or that some person disobeyed authority. There are many cases in antiquity of priests who disobeyed their bishop.

Against these we have the overwhelming evidence from all parts of the Church for the Roman primacy, as clear as we have it for the authority of a bishop in his own diocese.

So we come to evidence for our first thesis down to the year 451.

1. *The Pope is the chief bishop, primate and leader of the whole Church of Christ on earth.*

This is contained again a fortiori in our later theses. Meanwhile, taking this point alone, we have in the first century two expressions of St. Ignatius, the martyr-bishop of Antioch (d. c. 107). He speaks of "the presiding Church in the place of the land of the Romans", and he calls this Church the "president of the bond of love", meaning of the whole body of Christians, if we accept Funk and Harnack's translation.[1] In the second century the epitaph of Abercius of Hieropolis says that the Shepherd "sent me to Rome, that I might see the palace and the queen with a golden dress and golden shoes. I saw there a people having a splendid

---

[1] Ἥτις καὶ προκάθηται ἐν τό πω χωρίου Ῥωμαίων ... προκαθημένη τῆς ἀγάπης, salutation of St. Ignatius in his epistle to the Romans. Funk translates: "Quæ etiam præsidet in loco regionis Romanorum ... universo caritatis coetui præsidens" (*Patres apost.* [Tübingen, 1901], I, p. 253). He shows that προκάθηται is not to be taken with χωρίου but absolutely "the presiding Church". The rest shows where this church is. Προκαθημένη, etc., is sometimes translated as "distinguished in charity". But that would require the dative, not genitive. Ignatius uses ἀγάπη for the Church several times (e.g., Trall. XIII, I), and there are exact parallels to the phrase (Theodoret calls Rome τῆς οἰκουμένης προκαθημένην, "presiding over the world", Ep. 113; see Funk, loc. cit.). Harnack: "However much one may tone down all excessive expressions in his letter to the Romans, this much is clear, that Ignatius has admitted in fact a precedence of the Roman community in the circle of her sisters, and that he knows of an energetic and perpetual activity on the part of this community in supporting and teaching others.... Even the elaborate address shows that he honours and greets this community as the most distinguished in Christendom" (*Dogmengesch.* IV, ed. 1909, p. 486 and note 2).

seal".[2] If this inscription is Christian, as most authorities agree,[3] it implies clearly preeminence of the Church of Rome. St. Irenaeus (d. c. 202) has a passage[4] enormously discussed, as everyone knows. The discussion turns on its second part, of which later. For our present thesis we have, at any rate, the undeniable fact that he calls Rome "the greatest, most ancient Church, known to all" and says that this Church has a "mightier rule".

In the third century we come to St. Cyprian (d. 258). It is strange that Cyprian is invoked, with equal persistence, by both defenders and opponents of the papacy. On the one hand, we find in him some of the plainest expressions of the Roman primacy. On the other hand, there are cases when he quarrelled with the Pope and resisted his orders. Perhaps we may as well say something (in the limit of our space) about these cases at once. Cyprian was very much annoyed when the party of Novatus and Felicissimus, rebellious priest and deacon of Cyprian's province, at last persuaded Pope Cornelius (251–253) to admit them to communion.[5] He protests to the Pope against this.[6] He thought that, in this matter of discipline, his brother of Rome was taking the wrong side. There is also here a sign of the strong dislike of the Africans to appeals by the lower clergy

---

[2] Vers. 7–8. In E. Preuschen, *Analecta* (Freiburg and Leipzig: Mohr, 1893), p. 26.

[3] Preuschen, Harnack, Bardenhewer, Pitra, Ramsay, Lightfoot, de Rossi, T. Zahn and others.

[4] *Adversus hæreses*, L. III, c. 3, no. 2 (ed. Stieren, pp. 428–30).

[5] Cornelius drove them away at first but yielded finally to their importunity. It is a pity he did.

[6] Ep. LIX. Some people may be surprised that Cyprian calls the Pope his brother. In the first line of this letter, he calls Saturus, an acolyte, his brother.

to Rome, over the head of their bishops and primate. This feeling found its expression later, notably in the seventeenth canon of the Synod of Carthage, in 418.[7] In his letter to Cornelius, Cyprian states his case against the rebellious clergy and complains of the way they have been received by the Pope. He thinks that at this rate, there would be an end of any proper authority of local bishops. There is nothing in his letter that denies the primacy of Rome. He is only protesting against what he considers its misuse in one case. Moreover, this very letter contains one of his strongest statements for the primacy. The other case is Cyprian's attitude about heretical baptism. Here, undoubtedly, he resisted the Pope's rule, and in his synod of 256 he persuaded all the African bishops to take his side. No one now denies that in the main issue St. Cyprian was wrong, that the Pope took the right view theologically, as it is also more charitable. It is worth noting that in this case, as in so many, Rome took the tolerant, reasonable position and opposed strongly just what many Protestants would suppose to be Popish intolerance. All Christendom has accepted the Pope's view.[8] St. Cyprian and his friend Firmilian of Caesarea were wrong in the main question, so there is no great difficulty in understanding how, in defending that wrong view, they disagreed with the Pope. The pity is that so great a saint should for once have fallen into the usual attitude of heretics, namely, to disobey the Pope's authority, in denying

---

[7] Priests, deacons and lower clerks are to carry their cases to bishops of their province, or to the primate, not to a tribunal beyond the sea (Hefele-Leclercq, II, p. 195). Bishops are not included in this law (Ballerini, *S. Leonis opp.*, III, p. 963).

[8] Except some of the Orthodox, who think no sacraments valid outside the true (their own) church. They rebaptize Anglicans; we do not.

the truth that the Pope defended. But the question was, at any rate directly, one of discipline rather than of faith; and Cyprian had this much excuse, that many heretical baptisms are invalid for want of form. The quarrel was made up before the martyr's glorious death; the Roman Church in her canon names Cyprian, almost the only foreigner,[9] among her own martyrs. In no case does St. Cyprian deny the Roman primacy, not even when, in a matter of discipline, he went his own mistaken way. He does affirm it repeatedly.[10] He knows that there is "one Church and one see, founded by the Lord's voice on Peter. No other altar can be set up, no new priesthood be made, except the one altar and one priesthood. Whoever gathers elsewhere scatters."[11] There is "one Church founded by Christ our Lord on Peter, by the source and reason of unity".[12] He knows that the Bishop of Rome is successor of St. Peter and inheritor of Peter's primacy: "Cornelius was made bishop ... when the place of Fabian [Pope, 236–260], that is, when the place of Peter and the [high] degree of the priestly throne was vacant."[13] The Roman see is the "mother and root of the Catholic Church".[14] The African schismatics "dare to set

---

[9] Except Cosmas and Damian (who, however, had a strong local cult at Rome) and, of course, our Lady (and since the intervention of John XXIII in 1962, St. Joseph) and the apostles in the *Communicantes* list. The *Nobis quoque* list has foreigners.

[10] The best attack on this statement is Hugo Koch, *Cyprian u. der römische Primat* (Leipzig: Hinrichs, 1910). He is well answered by Anton Seitz, *Cypr. u. der röm. Primat* (Regensburg: Manz, 1911).

[11] Ep. LXIII, 5 (ed. Hartel, p. 594).

[12] Ep. LXX, 3 (ibid., p. 769).

[13] Ep. LV, 8 (ibid., pp. 629–30): "Cum locus Petri et gradus cathedræ sacerdotalis vacaret."

[14] "Ecclesiæ catholicæ matricem et radicem", Ep. XLVIII, 3 (ibid., p. 607).

sail and bring letters to the throne of Peter and the chief Church, whence priestly unity came forth".[15]

Emperor Constantine knew who was the chief bishop of Christendom. When the Donatist troubles began in Africa, he ordered the schismatics to go to Rome, to be judged by the Pope (Melchiades, 310–314). They wanted Gauls to examine their case, so he told three Gallic bishops to join the Pope's court as assessors (313).[16] The Donatists would not accept the verdict of this Roman court, to Constantine's great annoyance,[17] so the next year (314), he summoned another synod at Arles; Pope Silvester I sent his legates. This Council sends its finding to the "most glorious Pope", regrets that he was not able to be present and begs him "who holds the greater dioceses"[18] to tell all the other bishops its verdict.[19] Down to 451 four general councils were held. The second of these is counted as such only through the later acceptance of the Church. The Pope presided through his legate at the three others. At Nicea (325)

---

[15] Ep. LIX, 14 (ibid., p. 683). The antipapal answer to this is that Cyprian means only the chief Church in the West, whence came unity to Africa (he says neither); that he was concerned only with Cornelius' claim to be Bishop of Rome against Novatian (that Cornelius was lawful bishop would not make his see *ecclesiæ catholicæ matrix et radix*); that St. Peter was the apostle first called, first in that sense only (Peter was not the first called; Andrew was); that the one see founded on Peter is the collective episcopate (this is not one see and was not founded on Peter); and such like. People who have no special axe to grind admit willingly that Cyprian acknowledges the Roman primacy (e.g., Harnack, *Dogmengesch.*, ed. cit. I, 493).

[16] Constantine's letter is in Eusebius, *Hist. Eccl.* X, cap. 5, nos. 18–20. The Pope is to conduct the matter.

[17] "They demand judgment from me, who myself await the judgment of Christ" (C.S.E.L. XXVI, p. 209).

[18] "Qui maiores dioceses tenes", a strange phrase. Hefele suggests "maioris dioceseos gubernacula" (ed. cit. I, 279).

[19] C.S.E.L. XXVI, pp. 206–8.

Hosius of Cordova "held the place of the Bishop of Rome, with the priests Vito and Vincent".[20] He presided and signed first "in the name of the Church of Rome, the Churches of Italy, Spain and the West".[21]

Optatus of Milevis (c. 370), who is known for his opposition to Donatism, wrote:

> On the one throne, which is first in gifts,[22] Peter sat first, to whom succeeded Linus [a list of Popes to his own time follows].... To Damasus succeeded Siricius, who is our comrade today, with whom, together with us, the whole world agrees in the society of one communion, by exchange of letters.[23]

Again (this to the Donatists): "How can you pretend to have the keys of the Kingdom of Heaven, who sacrilegiously fight against the see of Peter by your presumption and impudence?"[24] The First Council of Constantinople (381), anxious to magnify the new Imperial city, recognizes formally that old Rome is the first see and asks only that new Rome be second after her.[25] The Synod of Aquileia in 381, of which St. Ambrose was the guiding spirit, though not president, tells the emperors that the "Roman Church is the head of the whole Roman world",[26] not merely of the West. The Roman world then contained the whole Church.[27]

---

[20] Gelasius of Cyzicus, in Mansi, II, 805.

[21] Mansi, II, 692, 697.

[22] "Prima de dotibus", first in the gifts Christ gives to his Church.

[23] "Commercio formatarum." *Formatæ* (*epistolæ*) are letters of intercommunion between bishops. Opt. Mil. II, c. 3.

[24] Ibid., II, 5.

[25] Can. 3.

[26] Ambrosi, Ep. XI, 4.

[27] Except Armenia and East Syria, of which these Fathers could hardly have heard.

Next year a synod was again held at Constantinople (382). The Fathers here assembled send their decision to the Pope and his synod at Rome for their approval; they say that they have met together according to what the Romans had written.[28] The pagan Ammianus Marcellinus (fourth century) knows who is the chief bishop of the Christians. Pope Liberius has "that authority by which the bishops of the eternal city are more mighty".[29] St. Jerome (d. 419) says that even dumb beasts have their chiefs; there can be only one emperor (he is wrong there, by the way), only one judge of a province. "In a ship is only one man at the wheel, in a house one master, in an army, however great, the banner of one is followed." So it must be in the Church.[30] But St. Jerome, as most of the Fathers, will occur again more definitely, when we come to our further points. The great St. Augustine (d. 430) stated that "in which [the Roman Church] the ruling authority of the Apostolic See has always held firm."[31] The Fathers at Ephesus (431) were "summoned by the holy canons and by the letter of our holy father and fellow-minister Celestine (Pope, 422–443)."[32] According to Philip, papal legate at Ephesus,

> There is no doubt, indeed it is known to every age, that the holy and most blessed Peter, prince and head of the apostles, column of faith and foundation of the Catholic Church, received the keys of the Kingdom from our Lord Jesus Christ, Savior and Redeemer of the human race, that to him was given power of forgiving and retaining sins,

---

[28] Mansi, III, 582.

[29] Amm. Marc. XV, c. 7, no. 10 (Teubner, 1874, p. 63).

[30] Ep. 125, ad Rusticum, no. 15 (PL XXII, 1080).

[31] Ep. 43, no. 7 (PL XXXIII, 163).

[32] Mansi, IV, 1287.

who [Peter] to this time and always lives and judges in his successors.[33]

The bishops of the province of Arles write to Pope Leo I (440–461) that "through blessed Peter, prince of the apostles, the most holy Roman Church should hold sovereignty over all the Churches of the whole World."[34] Emperor Marcian (450–457), arranging for the Council of Chalcedon, writes to Pope Leo I: "By the synod to be held, thou being the author, the greatest peace shall obtain among all bishops of the Catholic faith."[35] His wife, St. Pulcheria, uses the same expression; she hopes that the bishops will decide "as faith and Christian piety require, thou being the author".[36] Chalcedon in 451 brings us to the end of our period. The difficulty was not to find texts to prove this first thesis but to avoid those that we shall need for the more far-reaching ones that will follow. We have chosen some of the most obvious from the mainstream of Christian life in this period. The outlying Churches agree. When the Armenians, under their king, Vartan, were in great fear of the Persians, they sent for help to Emperor Theodosius II (408–450). Their claim on him is that the Persians will "destroy among us the faith we received from the prince of bishops, who is at Rome".[37] Among the Syrians, Narses of Nisibis sings that "the prince of the disciples obtained the mother-city, and placed the eyes of faith in her as in

---

[33] Mansi, IV, 1294.

[34] PL LIV, 881.

[35] Σοῦ αὐθεντοῦντος, "under thy authority", PL LIV, 899.

[36] Ibid., 907.

[37] Quoted in Fr. Tournebize, *Hist. pol. et rel. de L'Arménie* (Paris, 1900), p. 80.

the head." [38] Yeshu'yab of Chadyab (Adiabene) says: "Let him become the chief of Rome, according to the order of the apostles, which they have established in their ecumenical canons. The precedence and primacy of the Patriarchate have been given to mighty Rome." [39] But we have wandered beyond our appointed limit. Yeshu'yab became Nestorian Katholikos in 650. All the same, the Nestorians had certainly not learned this since they went out from the Catholic Church after Ephesus.

---

[38] Quoted in G. E. Khayyath, *Syri orientales et Rom. Pont. primatus* (Rome, 1870), p. 41.

[39] C. B. Benni, *The Tradition of the Syrian Church* (Burns, Oates and Co., 1871), p. 84 (text, Syr. no. 121, at end p. 53—Syr. numbering).

5

The Pope's Jurisdiction

Our second thesis is: *The Pope has episcopal jurisdiction over all members of the Church.* This is the vital matter of all, more vital really than infallibility. It is also the thesis for which there are the most convincing witnesses from the first four and a half centuries. The witnesses here are of two kinds; first, there are texts of Fathers, decisions of councils that say so; second, there are even more striking proofs from cases where this jurisdiction was used, where a Pope decides a question, and his decision is accepted, in a way that can be understood only on the supposition that his universal jurisdiction was admitted by all Catholics. We consider both kinds of evidence together.

The first case is one that we must describe as astounding, unless we see in it the Providence of God, who intends that we should have what is perhaps the clearest example of the Pope's universal jurisdiction before the year 100. It is, of course, St. Clement's First Letter to the Corinthians. Toward the end of the first century the Christians of Corinth

rebelled against their hierarchy and drove out their presbyters.[1]
Thereupon "the Church of God dwelling at Rome" wrote
to "the Church of God dwelling at Corinth". In the first
place, this "Church of God at Rome" means the authority
of that Church, that is, her bishop. The only way to escape
this is to deny the monarchical rule of each Church at the
time; such a view would carry the Anglican further than
he would go. Moreover, there is constant tradition, from
Irenaeus down, that the letter was written by Clement,
Bishop of Rome.[2] Clement, in his letter, commands the
Corinthians to return to the obedience of their lawful hierarchy. He does not advise; he commands. He commands
with an authority, one would almost say with an arbitrary
tone, that has not been exceeded by any modern Pope. This
is what he says:

> If any disobey what he [Jesus Christ] says through us, let
> them know that they will be involved in no small offence
> and danger; but we shall be innocent of this sin.[3]

Again:

> You will give us joy and pleasure if you obey what we have
> written by the Holy Spirit.... We have sent trusty and wise
> men, who have lived without blame among us from youth
> to old age; these shall be witnesses between you and us. We
> have done so that you may know that all our care has been
> and is that you should soon be in peace.[4]

---

[1] Harnack, Funk, Bardenhewer, Lightfoot and Hilgenfeld, among others;
practically all authorities date the incident and the letter about the year 96
(under Emperor Nerva, 96–98).

[2] Irenaeus III, c. 3, no. 3; Hegesippus (Eus. HE IV, c. 22, no. 1); Dionysius Corinth. (ibid., IV, c. 23, g); Jerome, *de vir. ill.* 15, among others.

[3] 1 Clem. ad Cor. 59, 1.

[4] Ibid., 63, 2–4.

Consider the implications of this. Here we have a Bishop of Rome, the Church of Rome, if a man prefers to put it that way, assuming the right to send categorical orders to Christians in Greece. There is no question here of people in the Roman province—they are not even Italians; they live across the sea in a foreign land, for all practical purposes as far away as people in England. Yet to these Rome claims that she can command, that what she says is the voice of God himself to them. They must take, not advice, but commands; if they do not they are guilty of no small sin. Rome sends her legates to settle the dispute and enforce her commands. The Pope today could not claim authority over a distant diocese more uncompromisingly than this. And the date? This letter is written before the end of the first century. The bishop who writes it "saw the apostles themselves and lived with them".[5] His date is so early that his name occurs in the New Testament.[6] At the time he wrote, there is every probability that an apostle, St. John, was still alive at Ephesus. Yet it is not St. John but the Bishop of Rome who uses this jurisdiction over a distant Church. What does this mean but that already then, when the ink of St. Paul's epistles was scarcely dry, the Bishop of Rome has the care of all the Churches? Nor is there the slightest sign of objection to this jurisdiction. On the contrary, it is praised and quoted as an admirable document.[7] What protests such a letter would call forth from Protestants! The Corinthians had behaved badly to their clergy, but they were

---

[5] Iren. III, c. 3, no. 3.

[6] See Phil 4:3.

[7] Irenaeus calls it ἱκανωτάτη "befitting" (Eul. c.); Eusebius says it is μεγάλη καὶ θαυμασία "great and wonderful" (HE III, c. 16, no. 1), Dionysius of Corinth, that it is still read by the Church of Corinth (ibid., IV, c. 23, no. 11).

Catholics. The next thing we hear of them is that order is
restored in their Church.[8] The Pope's writ carried and was
obeyed in Greece within about sixty years from the death
of our Lord.

After such an example of papal jurisdiction at the very
beginning we shall not be surprised to find others in the
years that follow. Victor I of Rome (189–199) wished to
excommunicate the Quartodecimans of Asia.[9] This case is
often quoted against the primacy, because several Fathers,
including St. Irenaeus, protested against it. His letter should
be read.[10] He urges Victor not to insist on this; he says that
Victor's own predecessors had kept communion with people
who differed from them on a matter of mere discipline.
There is no hint that Victor cannot do what he threatens.
On the contrary, Eusebius' text is clear: Victor meant to
cut these people in Asia off, not only from his own communion, but from the unity of the whole Church.[11] In face
of this opposition Victor changed his mind. Either he never
published the excommunication or he withdrew it at once.[12]
All the same, we have again the situation that a Bishop of
Rome in the second century claims the right to use real
jurisdiction over Christians in Asia—that no one denies his
claim, though they thought he had better not do so in this
case. In view of the controversy around this incident, we
may note further that Rome was right in the root of the

---

[8] From Hegesippus, about sixty years later (Eus. HE IV, c. 22, no. 2).

[9] Who had their own tradition for the dating of Easter.

[10] In Eus. HE V, c. 24, nos. 12–17.

[11] Ἀποτέμνειν τῆς κοινῆς ἑνώσεως πειρᾶται, "He attempted at one stroke
to sever from unity", Eus. HE V, c. 24, no. 9.

[12] This is the force of Eusebius' πειρᾶται "attempted". Victor intended to
do it but did not.

matter, and her view has been accepted ever since by all. There are no Quartodecimans now.

Pope Zephyrinus (199–217) cast the African Montanists out of the Church. Tertullian (d. c. 220) was a Montanist, so he is bitterly angry with the Pope. He says that, so far, the Roman Bishop had "brought peace to the Church of Asia and Phrygia" (again universal jurisdiction) but that now he had revoked his letters.[13]

> I hear that an edict is proposed, and a peremptory one. Namely, the Supreme Pontiff, that is the Bishop of bishops, says: I will forgive sins of adultery and fornication to those who do penance for them.[14]

This is Tertullian in bitter irony. After his fall he does not acknowledge the Bishop of Rome as Supreme Pontiff and Bishop of bishops; but he means that something of the kind is held by his opponents who are the Catholics. His argument against the Pope further shows that the Pope claimed the authority of St. Peter as prince of the apostles.[15] Pope Callistus (217–222) made a decree about the deposition of other bishops, showing that he claimed jurisdiction in the matter.[16] St. Cyprian (d. 258) asks Pope Stephen I (254–257) to intervene in the affair of Marcian, bishop of Arles, who was a Novatian; he urges the Pope to excommunicate this heretic and to see to it that a Catholic bishop be appointed.[17] He himself does not excommunicate but asks the Pope to do so. In the cases of his own rebels Basilides and Martial, he

---

[13] *Adv. Prax.*, I.

[14] *De Pudic.*, I.

[15] Ibid., 21. An early case of *Tu es Petrus*, "Thou art Peter", quoted by a Pope.

[16] *Philosophumena* IX, 12.

[17] Ep. 68, 3 (C.S.E.L. III, pp. 745–46).

begs Pope Cornelius (251–253) not to accept their appeal.[18] There is no suggestion here that the Pope has no authority to do so; on the contrary, by his anxiety to warn Cornelius against these men, he implies that Cornelius could. Soon after the death of Pope Fabian (250), the clergy of Rome heard that St. Cyprian had abandoned his flock in the persecution. At once they wrote to their brother clergy in Africa, to warn them about this.[19] Again we read in this letter most striking expressions of authority over members of a distant Church. "We, who are the chiefs, have the duty of keeping the flock in the place of the shepherds."[20] The flock in question is the Church of Africa, to whom they sent not merely advice, but commands: "You must" do so and so, throughout the letter. "Your brethren who are in prison, and the priests, and the whole Church, who watches with the greatest care over all who call on the name of the Lord, greet you"[21]—again this same tone of authority and the same sense of responsibility for all. Only one local Church claims that it is her duty to watch over all who call on the name of the Lord.

When Denis of Alexandria was suspect of false doctrine, some members of his diocese went to Rome and denounced him to Denis of Rome (259–269). The Pope wrote to his namesake to hear his side of the case; Denis of Alexandria "cleared himself" and all was well.[22] Here is a man, a very great man indeed, for he was the second patriarch in

---

[18] Ep. 67 (ibid., pp. 735–43).

[19] Among St. Cyprian's letters, no. 8.

[20] Ep. 8, I (C.S.E.L. III, p. 486). The Roman see was vacant at the moment; these priests act like the College of Cardinals *sede vacante* ("the see being vacant") now.

[21] Ibid., no. 3 (p. 488).

[22] So St. Athanasius: *Ep. de sent. Dionysi*, 13 (PG XXV, 499).

Christendom, suspect and accused. Where is he accused?
At Rome; he defends himself to the one bishop who was a
greater man than he. If the Roman Bishop has the right to
judge a patriarch of Alexandria, then no Catholic is too
great, no country too distant to escape his authority. St.
Athanasius was also patriarch of the second see in Christendom and was a greater man than his predecessor. As far
as influence went, he was in his time by far the greatest
man of all. For over forty years the name of Athanasius was
the rallying point of Catholics against Arianism. Athanasius, too, submitted to the jurisdiction of the Pope. He was
denounced to Pope Julius I (337–352). Socrates says:

> When they[23] had explained their cause to Julius, Bishop of
> the city of Rome, he sent them back to the East strength-
> ened by free letters, and restored to each his see, as is the
> right of the Roman Church.[24]

So also Sozomenus: "Since the care of all was his affair,
because of the rank of his see, he gave back to each his
own Church."[25] Julius himself writes to the Eastern bishops: "Do you not know that this is the custom, that first
you must write to us, and that here what is just shall be
decreed";[26] again: "It is not right to make laws for the
Churches apart from the knowledge of the Bishop of
Rome."[27]

We come to the famous Council of Sardica in 344, so
often quoted as Nicea. It was not Nicea; it was not a general

---

[23] Athanasius and four other bishops accused with him.
[24] Socr. HE II, 15 (PG LXVII, 211).
[25] Soz. HE III, 8 (PG LXVII, 1051).
[26] *Ep. ad orient.*, in Athanasius, *Apol. c. Arian.*, 21 (PL VIII, 905 seq.).
[27] Socr. II, 17.

council, but it is one more witness for its time. Its third canon formally approves of the right of appeal to the Pope by any bishop, "that we may honour the memory of the apostle Peter"; its fourth declares that a deposed bishop who has appealed to Rome is not to be given a successor until the Pope has judged the matter; the fifth arranges the manner of the Pope's revision of a bishop's trial, either by appointing the neighboring bishops to examine it or by sending his own legates.[28] The council then writes to Julius: "It seemed best and most proper that the priests of the Lord[29] should refer from every province to the head, that is to the see of the Apostle Peter." [30] It is difficult to understand how anyone can dispute that the canons of Sardica in 344 recognize the jurisdiction of the Pope over all other bishops.[31]

---

[28] Hefele-Leclercq, *Hist. des Conc.* I (2), pp. 762–70.

[29] "Domini sacerdotes", bishops, as always.

[30] Ep. syn. Sard. ad Iul. (Harduin, I, 653).

[31] Mr. F. W. Puller, however, manages to deny this. He thinks Sardica a great argument *against* the papacy, because it was a new law introduced by Hosius tentatively (*si vobis placet*, "if you please"); it conferred what Roman Catholics say already belonged to the Pope by divine right; it gave a very limited jurisdiction in one case only, to him who claims universal jurisdiction in all cases; it was never really received by the East (*The Primitive Saints and the See of Rome*, Lect. IV, 3rd ed. [London: Longmans, 1914], pp. 140–44; append. E, pp. 172–77). That the canons of Sardica were not a new law is proved by the appeals to Rome before this synod, of which some are quoted in this article. Synods constantly repeat and enforce what is already ancient law, as can. 2 of Nicea forbids a neophyte to be ordained bishop (already forbidden by 1 Tim 3:6). The words *Si placet* are the regular conventional form in proposing a motion to synods; they never have any restrictive force (see Hefele-Leclercq, loc. cit., p. 771, and Nat. Alexander quoted there). What is proposed to the synod "an it please you" is not whether the Pope has this jurisdiction (he had it already) but whether the Fathers think it well to pass this particular canon at the moment. So in any modern synod, a bishop might propose: "Does it please you that we assert our belief in the Holy Trinity, in view of the prevalence of Unitarianism in the country?"

To receive an appeal and revise a trial is the plainest possible case of jurisdiction. These canons became common law in the East and West. In the West they were incorporated into the *Corpus iuris canonici*;[32] in the East they were confirmed by the Synod of Constantinople in Trullo (692),[33] otherwise so unfriendly to Rome.

The Far Eastern Churches (Assyrians, Jacobites, Copts, Armenians and so forth) have a collection of eighty-four alleged canons of Nicea[34] in Arabic. That these are genuine pronouncements of the Council in 325 we do not claim. They seem a compilation from several sources, among others from Sardica. At any rate, they are old enough to come within our period.[35] Canon 44 of this collection says:

> As the Patriarch has power over his subjects, so also the Roman Pontiff has power over all Patriarchs; as Peter had [power] over all the princes of Christendom and over their

---

Further, by making a special law about appeals, in view of an urgent case (Athanasius' deposition at Tyre, and so forth), the synod does not deny other matters on which it does not touch. But this special law does imply papal jurisdiction over all bishops. It does not give this jurisdiction as a new gift; it confirms one case of the Pope's jurisdiction by its own authority, as it confirms the fifth canon of Nicea by its own thirteenth, as innumerable synods have taken up and repeated some special point of already extant law, in danger of being forgotten. It is not true that the East did not accept the canons of Sardica; the exact contrary is true. But in any case, this does not affect the value of its witness.

[32] "The corpus of canon law". In the *Versio hispanica* (fourth century), they follow the canons of Nicea, with which they were often confused. They occur in all the other collections and are quoted eight times by Gratian, the twelfth-century canonist.

[33] Can. 2.

[34] According to the text of Abraham Echellensis (published at Paris in 1645); see Mansi, II, col. 1071.

[35] On the Arabic canons of Nicea, see Hefele-Leclercq I, (i), pp. 511–20. They are the translation of a Greek text drawn up perhaps in the fifth century.

councils, because he is the Vicar of Christ over redemption, over the Churches, and over the people committed to him.[36]

This may stand as the witness of the Far East in our period.

In the time of St. Basil (bishop of Caesarea, 370–379), the East[37] was torn by schisms, heresy and troubles of all kinds. He writes to Pope Damasus in 371:

> Our only hope is in a visitation from Your Clemency. Send us men who share our faith. They will settle quarrels, they will bring union to the Churches of God; at least they will make known to you the authors of the troubles, so that you will know whom to admit to your communion.[38]

Then he writes to Athanasius:

> We thought we ought to write to the Bishop of Rome, that he should examine our affairs ... that he should use authority in the matter, choosing men fit to bear the toil of the journey, fit also gently and firmly to correct the perverse among us.[39]

A Roman synod under Damasus in 378 writes to the emperors Gratian and Valentinian II:

> Certain bishops, unworthy pastors, have carried their insolence and contempt to the point of refusing obedience to the Bishop of Rome.

---

[36] Harduin I, 485, cf. can. 71 (ibid., 491).

[37] He says "from Illyricum to Egypt" in this letter (Ep. 70).

[38] Ep. 70 (PG XXXII, 435).

[39] Ep. 69, I (ibid., 431).

If the accused is himself a Metropolitan, he will be ordered to go at once to Rome, or in any case to appear before the judges whom the Bishop of Rome shall appoint.[40]

St. Ambrose and other bishops of Italy, writing to Theodosius about the affair of Antioch (381), remind him that "Athanasius and Peter, Bishops of Alexandria, and many Easterns, appealed to the judgment of the Church of Rome, of Italy and of all the West." [41] The Council of Milan under Ambrose (c. 389) applauds the condemnation of the heretic Jovinian by Pope Siricius (384–399):

We see in the letter of Your Holiness the vigilance of a good shepherd keeping faithfully the gate entrusted to you, watching over the fold of Christ with holy care, worthy that the sheep of the Lord should hear and follow you.[42]

Pope Siricius in 385 writes to Himerius of Tarragona:

We bear the burden of all who are laden; or rather the blessed Apostle Peter bears them in us, who, as we trust, will protect us the heirs of all his government.[43]

Innocent I praises the Council of Carthage in 417 that it has "kept and confirmed the example of ancient discipline":

You have referred to our judgment, knowing what is due to the Apostolic See, from which the episcopate itself and all authority of this name has come.... You know that nothing even in the most distant provinces is to be settled until

---

[40] Mansi, III, 624 *seq.*, PL XIII, 575. Cf. Martin Rade, *Damasus, Bischof von Rom* (Tübingen: Mohr, 1882), pp. 34–37.

[41] Ambr., Ep. 13, no. 4.

[42] Ambr., Ep. 42, no. 1. The "fold of Christ" is not only the diocese of Rome. The bishops at Milan count themselves among the sheep (no. 14).

[43] Ep. 1 (PL XIII, 1133).

it comes to the knowledge of this see; so that the decision
be established by the whole authority of this see.[44]

Pope Zosimus in 418, to the African bishops, again appeals
to the tradition of the Fathers, which teaches that "our
authority is so great that no one can contradict our decision."[45] St. Jerome remembers the care of Rome for all
Churches when "many years ago, when I assisted Damasus,
Bishop of the city of Rome, in writing letters, and had to
answer consultations from synods in East and West."[46]
Augustine proves the authority of Caecilian of Carthage from
his being "united by letters of communion to the Roman
Church, in which the supreme authority of the Apostolic
throne has always been held".[47] The words of the Roman
legate at Ephesus in 431 claim universal jurisdiction for his
bishop.[48] Leo I (440–461) says:

> The order of truth remains; blessed Peter, keeping the
> strength of the rock, does not abandon the helm of the
> Church. Whatever we do rightly is his work, whose power
> lives in his see.[49]

> In the person of my lowliness he is seen, he is honoured, in
> whom remains the care of all pastors and of the sheep of
> their charge. His power does not fail, even in an unworthy
> heir.[50]

---

[44] Innoc. I., Ep. 29, no. 1 (PL XX, 582–83).
[45] Ep. 12 (PL XX, 676).
[46] Ep. 123, ad Ageruchiam, no. 10 (PL XXII, 1052).
[47] Ep. 43, c. 3, no. 7 (PL XXXIII, 163).
[48] Quoted above, pp. 61–62.
[49] Serm. III, c. 2 (PL LIV, 145–46).
[50] Ibid., c. 4 (ibid., 147–48).

St. Peter Chrysologus of Ravenna (d. c. 450) writes to
Eutyches:

> I exhort you in all things, honoured brother, to attend obe-
> diently to what is written by the most blessed Pope of the
> Roman city; for St. Peter, who lives and reigns in his own
> see, will help those who seek the truth.[51]

Theodoret of Kyrrhos (d. 458) writes to Leo I:

> I await the sentence of your Apostolic See; I beg and implore
> Your Holiness to help me who appeal to your right and
> just tribunal to send for me to you, that I may show that
> my doctrine agrees with the tradition of the apostles....
> Above all I beg you to tell me whether I am to submit to
> this unjust deposition or not. I await your sentence.[52]

There is much more evidence, from Gelasius I (492–496),
and so on, to the Formula of Hormisdas[53] and to that most
practical acknowledgment of the Pope's jurisdiction sup-
plied by Photius when he appealed to Rome in 857. But
Leo I brings us again to the year of Chalcedon and the
limit we have set ourselves. These texts from synods and
Fathers of the East and West agree that the Popes had, used,
were acknowledged to have, and were obeyed in using real
jurisdiction over patriarchs and bishops of the whole Church.

---

[51] Among Leo I's letters, Ep. 25, no. 2 (PL LIV, 741).

[52] Ep. 113 (PG LXXXIII, 1315).

[53] The Formula used at the time of Pope Hormisdas (515) as the basis of
reconciliation with Rome after the Acacian schism which owes its importance to the great number of bishops in the East and West who signed it. Cf.
Adrian Fortescue, *The Formula of Hormisdas* (London: CTS, 1914).

6

Communion with Rome

Third thesis: *To be a member of the Catholic Church, a man must be in communion with the Pope.* This follows from what we have already said about papal jurisdiction. If the Pope has jurisdiction over all members of the Church, they must all be in communion with him.[1] It follows from the still more radical principle that members of the Catholic Church necessarily are in communion with one another, as we have explained. If this is admitted, and it is admitted that the chief bishop is certainly himself a member, then our thesis follows as a matter of course.

The necessity of communion between all members of the Catholic Church is the fundamental point on which every Anglican, however High he may be, must and does

---

[1] It would not be quite exact to say that no one can ever use jurisdiction over a man not in communion with himself. There are cases where, for a fresh offense, the Pope has pronounced a fresh sentence of excommunication against someone who had already broken communion with him. However, the normal, peaceful use of jurisdiction (which is what Church law contemplates) obviously supposes communion between authority and subject.

differ from us. Once more, let Catholics always remember
this first point of all. The Anglican invariably tries to avoid
or ignore it and to turn the discussion to the papal claims.
It is a pity that sometimes his Catholic opponent allows
him to drift away from the essential question. The visible
unity of the Church of Christ is the root of all our belief,
after the existence of God, the claim of Christ as our teacher,
and the fact that Christ did found a Church. All else (including the papacy) we believe because the Church of Christ
teaches it, relying on his promises to her. But we cannot get
any further toward knowing what the Church teaches till
we know what the Church is. The whole principle of believ-
ing the teaching of the Church goes by the wayside, if we
admit the possibility that the Church may consist of a group
of separate communions, all teaching something different.
In this case you have to take the greatest common measure
of the teachings of various churches picked out arbitrarily.
All idea of divinely given authority, divinely guided teaching, depends on the first concept of all, namely, one united
Church in communion with herself throughout the world.
Unhappily, here the extreme High Anglican is as remote
from us as any other Protestant. That is why his whole position is wrong and impossible. He copies our rites; he adopts
most points of our faith; he uses our language. But he does
not have the foundation on which all these things rest. He
is no nearer to us really, not one whit more Catholic, than
the Evangelical or the frank Protestant. We can leave all the
rest as of secondary importance till we have convinced him
of the one vital issue: the visible unity of the Church.

First, then, a few texts to prove that the Fathers down to
451 believed in unity of intercommunion between all members of the Catholic Church are essential. It was their direct
obvious test whether a man was a Catholic or not, just as it

is ours today. Schism meant to them what it means according to the plain sense of the word: breach of visible communion; and they said, as we say, that the schismatic is no Catholic.[2] This supposes that visible communion between all her members is an essential note of the Church; it is simply the note of unity, unless a man twist that note into some unnatural sense. Unless the Church is united as one society, by intercommunion among all her members, schism means nothing at all. According to the present Anglican theory, every Catholic is in schism with other Catholics.[3] That "schism" means breach of communion with the Catholics is too obvious to need much proof; it is what the word means. However, it so happens that the champion of the Catholic Church against the classical example of schism, Donatism, says this in so many words: "You schismatics, though you are not in the Catholic [Church] . . . it is manifest that you are schismatics, for you went out."[4]

The necessity of communion in the one society is seen in these texts. Irenaeus (d. c. 202) says:

No improvement can be made by them [schismatics] as great as is the evil of schism. He [the disciple] will judge all who are outside the truth—that is, who are outside the Church.[5]

---

[2] In view of further quibbling, by which people sometimes darken a simple issue, it may be well to state here that by "Catholic" we mean, and the Fathers always mean, a member of the Catholic Church, neither more nor less.

[3] He is, of course, in schism (that is, out of communion) with some people, with some (unhappily many) baptized Christians, namely, with all who are themselves heretics and schismatics. This was so from the beginning. The Fathers saw around them Arians, Monophysites, Novatianists and Donatists, with whom they were not in communion, just as we see Lutherans, Calvinists, Anglicans and Methodists.

[4] Optatus I, 12 (C.S.E.L. XXVI, pp. 14–15).

[5] Irenaeus IV, c. 33, no. 7 (Stieren, p. 670).

St. Cyprian (d. 258) says:

> Do they think the Christ will be with them when they are
> gathered up, who are gathered outside the Church of Christ?
> ... He is no martyr who is not in the Church.... They
> cannot remain with God who will not be of one mind in
> the Church of God.[6]

He is not speaking of persons unbaptized. He means baptized schismatics who "have gone out from us, when heresies and schisms were born later".[7] He knows that such
people have their own separate conventicles and appeal to
our Lord's words "wherever two or three are gathered in
my name"; but, he says, "The Lord speaks of his Church
and to those who are in his Church." That is why his words
do not apply to schismatics who have broken communion
with the one society.[8] It seems impossible that anyone could
read those chapters 10 to 15 of Cyprian's *On the Unity of
the Catholic Church* and fail to see that his whole point is
that there is, essentially, one communion, which is the
Church of Christ, that people not in this communion are
schismatics and not Catholics. He says the same thing in a
letter: "The Church which is Catholic and one is not broken nor divided; it is united and joined by the cement of
bishops who agree together."[9] In his time, there were
schismatic bishops (Novatian and Fortunatus, among others);
yet the Catholic Church is not divided: she is one in the
intercommunion of all her bishops. Novatian was a Roman
priest in the third century, then bishop in opposition to

---

[6] Cypr. *De cath. eccl. unitate*, 13–14 (C.S.E.L. III, 222).

[7] Ibid., 12, p. 220.

[8] Ibid., pp. 220–21.

[9] "Cohærentium sibi invicem sacerdotum glutino copulata" (Ep. LXVI, 8
[ibid., p. 733]).

Pope Cornelius (251–252). He had a large party in many countries, which lasted to the sixth century. The Novatianists[10] had as much right to consider themselves a branch of the Church, out of visible communion with other branches through unfortunate misunderstandings, as have Anglicans. St. Pacian (bishop of Barcelona, c. 360–390) does not take that view:

> Even if Novatian suffered[11] ... even if he was killed, yet he was not crowned. Why not? He was outside the peace of the Church, outside concord, outside that mother of whom he who is a martyr must be a part.[12]

Note again the "concord" as essential; the Church is one united communion. We have quoted Optatus of Milevis already.[13] He is a great authority on this matter, because his whole work is about the typical schism of the early Church. The idea of the unity of the Church—that schism is to be outside this unity (even if a man be baptized, even if he be no heretic), that schismatics are not members of the Church of Christ—occurs over and over again. This is his argument against the Donatists all the time. For instance:

> Simple and true understanding, one only and true sacrament, unity of souls make the Catholic [Church]. Schism is begotten when the cement of peace is broken ... when impious sons, having left the Catholic mother, go out and

---

[10] Novatian was scarcely a heretic. He was a rigorist in the matter of reconciling repentent apostates. He had many sympathizers in Gaul, Spain, Africa, Egypt and Asia. They had a schismatic hierarchy.

[11] He was said to have died a martyr.

[12] Ep. II, *Ad Sympronian.*, no. 7 (PL XIII, 1062).

[13] Cf. above, p. 60.

separate themselves, as you have done, are cut off from the
root of mother Church.[14]

St. Ambrose says:

> Perhaps there was there a church of the schism of that place
> [Sardinia]. For Lucifer [of Calaris] had then separated him-
> self from our communion. [Here we have Ambrose's defi-
> nition of schism: breach of communion.] Although Lucifer
> had been in exile for the faith and had left successors of his
> religion, yet he [Satyrus, Ambrose's brother] did not con-
> sider that faith was in a schism.[15]

So he looked out for a bishop in communion with the Pope,
as we shall see.

Such quotations as these prove our case in the best, most
essential way. One need not begin expressly by considering
the question of communion with the Pope (that will follow). The first thing is to consider what is meant by communion with the Church of Christ, which Church is
essentially one society, united, as is every society, by the
mutual recognition of all members. In Christianity this mutual
recognition is intercommunion. There is one such society,
visible to all men as one, a city set on a hill, whose obvious
unity throughout the world is the standing refutation of
absurd theories about a so-called one Church, which, however, consists of half a dozen separate churches, or of all
people who were once baptized, whatever they may have
become since, or about a visibility consisting only in the
fact that baptism is a visible sacrament. In this one Church,
as we have already seen, the Bishop of Rome is head on earth,
with authority over all her members. So every Catholic is

---

[14] Opt. Milev. I, 11 (C.S.E.L. XXVI, p. 14).
[15] *De excessu fratris sui Satyri*, I, no. 47 (PL XVI, 1306).

in communion with the Pope, because you cannot be in communion with the Church without being in communion with him.

But the Fathers do also constantly mention communion with the Pope directly, as the obvious and sufficient test. It is the same thing over again, in other words. They mention the Pope specially because he is the head on earth of the whole society. Union with the head is the obvious test to apply; it involves union with the other members, too.

We have mentioned Victor I (189–199) and have seen how, according to Eusebius, he understood that excommunication from himself meant excommunication from the whole Church.[16] We have also seen how St. Cyprian speaks of the "one Church and one see founded by the Lord's voice on Peter", that no one can make another altar or priesthood outside this. "Whoever gathers elsewhere scatters."[17] Twice he identifies communion with the Pope with membership in the Church: "That all our colleagues should prove and hold firmly to you [Pope Cornelius] and your communion, that is, to the unity and love of the Catholic Church";[18] to a Numidian bishop, Antonian, he states: "That he [Cornelius] might know that you are in communion with him, that is, with the Catholic Church."[19] The interpolation

---

[16] Eus. HE V, 24, 9; cf. above, p. 68.

[17] Ep. LXIII, 5; quoted above, p. 58.

[18] Ep. XLVIII, 3 (C.S.E.L. III, 607).

[19] Ep. LV, 1 (ibid., 624). The answer to this is that Cyprian means only that Cornelius, and not Novatian, is lawful Bishop of Rome, that Cornelius' communion at Rome is the Catholic one (Hugo Koch, *Cyprian u. der röm. Primat* [Leipzig: Hinrichs, 1910], 80–82). It is true that communion with any Catholic bishop is communion with the Catholic Church, for, as we have seen, in Cyprian's view all Catholic bishops are joined in one communion. So these two quotations might be placed in the earlier part of our article, before we come to Rome at all. We place them here, because, as a matter of

in Cyprian on the unity of the Church has: "He who leaves
the see of Peter, on which the Church is founded, can he
trust that he is in the Church? The Church is founded on
one."[20] Dom John Chapman has shown reason to believe
that these words were added by St. Cyprian himself.[21] In
any case, they are old; Pelagius II (579–590) quotes them.
At the time of the schism of Paul of Samosata, at Antioch,
when both parties were quarrelling over the use of a church,
the pagan emperor Aurelian (270–275) "most justly settled
this business, ordering that the building should be given to
those to whom the bishops of Italy and of the city of the
Romans should determine".[22] The test of Rome for Catholicity was known even to him. Optatus occurs again here. As
he was great on the essential unity of the Church, so was he
on communion with Rome as the criterion of this unity.
We have already quoted his text:

> You cannot deny that you know that the episcopal throne
> was set up by Peter in the city Rome ... in which one
> throne the unity is kept by all, that the other apostles might
> not each set up his own, that he would be a schismatic and
> a sinner who should set up another against the one throne.[23]

Again, when he speaks of the "one throne, which is first in
gifts" and gives a list of Popes to Pope Siricius, of his own

---

fact, he does speak of a Roman bishop and because the repeated insistence
on Rome implies a special perogative of that see. Cyprian nowhere uses this
language of another bishop. Just before the passage in Ep. XLVIII, 3, he has
called the Roman see "mother and root of the Catholic Church" (ibid.,
p. 607).

[20] De cath. eccl. unit. 4 (C.S.E.L. III, 212).

[21] That these are Cyprian's words has been firmly established by the subsequent scholarship of van den Eynde, Perler and Bévenot.

[22] Eusebius, HE VII, c. 30, no. 19.

[23] Opt. Mil. II, 2 (C.S.E.L. XXVI, p. 36).

time, he goes on, "who is our comrade today, with whom the whole world, with us, agrees in the society of one communion by the exchange of letters." [24] The Donatists, who are out of communion with the Pope, "by your presumption and insolence fight sacrilegiously against the throne of Peter".[25] "The whole world", of course, is a (common) poetic exaggeration. Optatus means the great Church throughout the world (though there were plenty of schismatic churches then, too). It would be difficult to reject the Anglican theory more plainly than by his definition of the Church as the society of one communion agreeing with the Pope.[26] Pope Siricius (384–399) not only claims that the Roman see is the head of the Churches of Spain, that all bishops of Spain and Africa must obey his commands, but he says that to be cut off from the communion of Rome is to be condemned to the pains of hell.[27] It is clearly to be outside the Church. Theophilus of Alexandria (385–412) writes to Flavian of Antioch: "Since we are in communion with the venerable Anastasius, Bishop of the Church of Rome, and since he leaves their rank to the clergy who gather apart [from Flavian] and is in communion with them, you see

---

[24] II, 3 (ibid., 37).

[25] II, 5 (ibid., 39).

[26] It is altogether false that Optatus means nothing more than that Siricius is lawful Bishop of Rome, instead of the Donatist antibishop. First he discusses the general question, the necessity of communion with the Pope (II, 2–3). Then, with a new beginning, he examines the Donatist answer to this (c. 4): "But you say that you also have a share in the city Rome" (namely, their schismatic bishop). He answers this objection: "This is a branch of your error, put forth by falsehood, not from the root of truth." It must surely be obvious to anyone reading the text honestly that c. 2–3 are not about the special objection that he picks up in c. 4 with a new beginning ("Sed et habere vos in urbe Roma partem aliquam dicitis").

[27] Ep. I, *ad Himerium* (PL XIII, 1133).

what follows",[28] namely, that these people are to be admitted. Again communion with the Pope is the test.

We have seen how St. Ambrose's brother, shipwrecked in Sardinia, feared the communion of a schismatic bishop. He knew how to make sure of avoiding that danger. "He sent for the bishop, nor did he think any grace true save that of the true faith, so he asked whether he were in communion with the Catholic bishops, *that is, with the Roman Church*."[29] So again St. Ambrose: "Where Peter is, there is the Church; where the Church is, there is no death, but eternal life."[30] Pope Boniface I (418–422) writes to the bishops of Thessaly: "It is therefore certain that this Church [the Roman see] is to the Churches throughout the world as the head to its members. If anyone cut himself off from this Church, not being in union with her, he is outside the Christian religion."[31] St. Augustine explains the authority of Caecilian of Carthage.

> [He has authority] because he saw himself joined by letters of communion to the Roman Church, in which the primacy of the apostolic see has always obtained, and with the other lands whence the Gospel had come to Africa.[32]

---

[28] Quoted from E. W. Brooks, *The Sixth Book of the Select Letters of Severus*, II, 302; by Cavallera, *Le Schisme d'Antioche*, p. 290; and J. Turmel, *Hist. du dogme de la Papauté* (Picard, 1908), p. 460. This letter is an incident in the movements to reconcile Flavian of Antioch, Meletius' successor, with the Pope; first Flavian must admit the Eustathian clergy to communion.

[29] *De excessu fratris sui Satyri*, I, 47 (PL XVI, 1306). Emphasis in original text.

[30] *Enarr. in Ps.* XL, no. 30 (PL XIV, 1082). He is explaining the text "Tu es Petrus", etc., and deduces this from "on this rock I will build my church." The Church is the communion of Peter. The Anglican answer to this is that the Church is where Peter is because Peter is a saint in heaven; of course, the Church is in heaven.

[31] Ep. XIV, episcopis per Thessaliam (PL XX, 777 B).

[32] Ep. XLIII, c. 3, no. 7 (PL XXXIII, 163).

When the Church of Antioch was distracted by the Meletian trouble, St. Jerome at Bethlehem writes to Pope Damasus:

> I speak with the successor of the fisherman and the disciple of the cross. I, who follow none but Christ as first, am joined in communion with Your Holiness, that is with the See of Peter. On this rock I know that the Church was built. Whoever eats the lamb outside this house is profane. Whoever is not in the ark of Noah will perish when the deluge comes. I know nothing of Vitalis, I defy Meletius, I care nothing for Paulinus. Whoever does not gather with you scatters; for whoever does not belong to Christ is of Antichrist.[33]

With these famous words of Jerome we may end our quotations for this thesis.

We have seen that, according to the Fathers before 451, the Church of Christ is one united communion; though in their time, too, there were many Christians outside her unity. These are schismatics; schismatics are not members of the visible Church. All Catholics are in mutual communion; but, since it would be long to count up all, the Fathers, as we do, appeal to the greatest, most ancient Church, known to all, founded by the two glorious apostles Peter and Paul at Rome. To them the obvious term of necessary communion is the chief bishop at Rome. Whom would these Fathers recognize as of their religion today—those who, like them, are joined in communion with the See of Peter, who speak with the successor of the fisherman; or those who eat the lamb outside this house, who are not in the ark, who say there is no one ark really, but a collection of boats all rowing different ways?

---

[33] Ep. XV, ad Damasum, 2 (PL XXII, 355–56).

7

Papal Infallibility

Our fourth and last thesis is: *The guidance of God will see to it that the Pope never commits the Church to error in any matter of religion.* This is the papal infallibility of the First Vatican Council. We have already explained what it means. The important point to understand is that this infallibility (in the sense of the Council) is a necessary, we might almost say an obvious, consequence of the Pope's universal jurisdiction, coupled with the infallibility of the Church. The Pope has jurisdiction in religious matters over the whole Church. We have seen that the early Fathers believed this. His jurisdiction is supreme and final. It applies to matters of faith as well as to discipline. The Holy See is the last court of appeal in the Church; the verdict of the last court of appeal must be accepted as final in any society. To this we add that God will always so guide the Church that she will not lead us into error. When we see that this infallibility of the Church was accepted, not only as a dogma but as the basis of all dogma, by the Fathers, we see that they held the whole theory of papal infallibility. It is the infallibility of the Church

that makes all the difference between the papacy and courts
of appeal in other societies. There are final courts of appeal
in the state also; yet no one claims that such courts are
infallible. Why not? Because no one holds that the state
itself is infallible. In the state, the decision of a final court
must be accepted as final. All the same, it may be wrong.
In this case we have only a kind of legal fiction. The verdict must be accepted as final, or there would be no end to
any trial. It is accepted as final in practice, although in theory
we admit that it may be mistaken. If it is, then the state
makes a mistake. But the Church cannot make a mistake in
her own business, because God has given her to us to be
our certain guide in religion, because our Lord promised
to guide her always and told us that in hearing his Church
we hear him. So the final verdict of the supreme court of
the Church cannot be mistaken about the faith. The infallibility of the Church rests upon the infallibility of Christ;
and the infallibility of the Church supposes the infallibility
of the Pope, if he has supreme jurisdiction in matters of
faith.

That the Fathers before 451 (as well as after that year)
believed that the *Church* is infallible is too obvious to require
many texts to prove it. This idea underlies all their appeal
to general councils, their demand that everyone must accept
as true what has been taught by the Church because it is so
taught, and their principle that a man who denies what the
Church teaches is a heretic, with whom they can have no
communion. In this matter, after our Lord himself, the first
Father we could quote is the Apostle St. Paul, "The Church
of the living God, pillar and ground of truth." [1] Another

---

[1] 1 Tim 3:15.

example is St. Irenaeus (d. c. 202): "Those who have the succession from the apostles have received a sure gift [*charisma*] of truth, according to the will of the Father."[2] Again:

Where the gifts [*charismata*] of the Lord are placed, there we must learn the truth, namely, from those who have the succession of the Church from the apostles. . . . These preserve our faith.[3]

We have not yet quoted St. Ephrem (d. 373). He may stand here as a witness from the East: "The heavenly spouse has established the Church and made her firm in the orthodox faith."[4] Not to take up too much space with what is obvious, we add one Father more—the greatest of all. St. Augustine says:

Unless the Lord dwelt in the Church, as she is now, the most careful speculation would fall into error; but of this Church is said: She is the holy temple of God.[5]

So the Church herself is infallible. To this we must add that, in the view of these same Fathers, the Bishop of Rome has final authority over her in matters of faith as well as of discipline. Some of the cases quoted already, as proofs of the Pope's supreme jurisdiction, are matters of faith. The affair of the Montanists excommunicated by Zephyrinus, of Denis of Alexandria, of Jovinian, of Eutyches and of others were questions of faith. In these, Popes decide with the same authority as in matters of discipline.

---

[2] *Adverses hæreses*, IV, c. 26, no. 2 (ed. Stieren, p. 645).

[3] Ibid., IV, c. 26, no. 5 (p. 647).

[4] *De instaur. eccl.* II, i (*Hymni et sermones*, ed. T.J. Lamy [Mechlin, 1886], tom. III, p. 966).

[5] In Ps. IX, no. 12 (PL XXXVI, 122).

Then we have texts in which this final, that is, infallible, authority of the Pope about faith is noted specially. Such texts are not all of the same value. Not every text, taken alone, proves papal infallibility. Sometimes a text only shows a man protesting that his faith is that of the Roman see. It is, of course, true that he might say this of any orthodox see. All the same, the repeated insistence on the fact that someone conforms with Rome, the at-least-implicit idea that this is what is wanted to establish his own orthodoxy, argues Rome as the final standard of right belief. Moreover, here, too, the weight of the evidence depends on the number of witnesses. It is not a case of one text only, but of the impression produced by a great number. To this impression each, in some way, adds its value. The point to note is not that one man says he agrees with Rome; a man might of course say this of any Catholic see; it is that so many, from East and West, all agree in appealing to the same see as test of their own faith. Other passages say much more than this, some that Rome is the standard for all, some that God will never allow the Roman Church to err in the faith. When we find this, we have papal infallibility in so many words.

Our first quotation must, naturally, be the famous text of St. Irenaeus. Probably no one sentence in all the works of the Fathers has been so much discussed as this. It is impossible to go adequately into that great controversy here. We must be content to quote, once more, the words[6] and to

---

[6] Iren. III, c. 3, no. 2 (Stieren, pp. 428–30). The Greek text of the work is lost, except for some quotations by Greek Fathers. We have only Latin versions from about the ninth century (cf. Stieren, pp. xi–xxiv). Many restorations of the Greek text have been attempted (one attempt in Stieren, under the Latin). Not much is lost by this, except for doubt about the article here and there. It is not difficult to see what the Greek must be. Whatever is ambiguous in the Latin would be equally so in Greek.

add a note about the chief points that occur. Irenaeus argues
against Gnostics from the tradition of the Church:

> But, since it would be very long to count up the succession
> of all Churches in such a book as this, by showing the tra-
> dition of the greatest and oldest[7] Church, known to all,
> founded and established by the two most glorious apostles,
> Peter and Paul, at Rome, which [tradition] she has from
> the apostles, and by showing the faith proclaimed to men
> through the series of her bishops down to us,[8] we con-
> found all who, in any way, gather beyond what is right,
> either to please themselves, or for vain glory, or by blind-
> ness and wrong opinion. For to this Church, because of
> her mightier rule,[9] every Church must agree [possibly: "to
> her must go"[10]], that is, those who are faithful from all

---

[7] "Oldest", *antiquissimæ*, ἀρχαιοτάτης, probably meaning "of greatest authority", as in II, c. 5, no. 4 (Stieren, p. 291). Origen uses the same expression
for the Church of Rome (in Eusebius, HE VI, c. 14, no. 10). Rome is not
the oldest Church in time, for Irenaeus knows that Antioch was founded
earlier (III, c. 12, no. 14).

[8] He gives the list of Popes from Linus to Eleutherius, his contemporary
(III, c. 3, no. 3), immediately after the words quoted.

[9] *Propter potentiorem* (*cod. claram.* potiorem) *principalitatem.*

[10] *Ad hanc . . . necesse est convenire*, πρὸς ταύτην . . . ἀνάγκη συμβαίνειν. *Convenire ad* is almost certainly συμβαίνειν πρός. It may mean either to "go to"
or "agree with". If we understand "agree with", we have Rome as the standard of faith most plainly. Many opponents of the papacy dismiss this meaning with scorn and suppose as obvious, "go to". Yet I believe it to be more
probably "agree with". If Irenaeus meant "go to", we should expect the *city*
Rome; but he says *Church*. Stieren (who is a Protestant) declares emphatically
for the meaning "agree with" (p. 430). So does Harnack: "Convenire is probably to be understood in its derived meaning; the literal and therefore more
obvious sense 'every Church must go to the Roman Church' is scarcely possible" (*Dogmengesch*, 1909, I, p. 487, n. 1). Irenaeus' argument is that the faith
of Rome is a sufficient criterion. This would not be proved by people going
to the city; it is proved by the necessity of all Churches agreeing with this
Church. Irenaeus constantly uses this, or a parallel word (*concurrere*), for agreement (II, c. 24, no. 3; II, c. 25, no. 2; IV, c. 36, no. 6, etc.). Similarly, in

sides, in which[11] the tradition from the apostles is kept by those who are from all sides.[12]

Taking the plain meaning of these words, we have that the Church of Rome has a mightier rule, and therefore every

---

English, "go along with" means "to agree". The only word that suggests the meaning "go to" is *undique*, πονταχόθεν (from all sides). But Stieren notes that Greeks often use adverbs of motion for simple adverbs of place (Stieren, p. 430, note b), and there is a sense of (intellectual) motion-from in agreement. Funk, on the whole, prefers "go to" (*Kirchengesch. Abhandl.* I, 15–21). In this case the idea is less obvious, but eventually it comes to the same thing. They go to Rome because of the mightier rule of that Church in which the tradition is kept.

[11] *In qua*. Does this refer to the Church at large (*omnem ecclesiam*, the last noun; so it would seem, so far, probably this), or to the Roman Church? If it is the Church at large, Irenaeus says that the faithful everywhere keep the faith, guarded by the mightier rule of Rome. If it is Rome, he says that the faith is kept there by the faithful from all places, who learn it at Rome from the Pope (this would support "go to" above). There is a third possibility. The text may be corrupt here. The second *undique*, so soon after the first, and in the same phrase repeated (*qui sunt undique*) seems suspicious. Is it a copyist's error? It has been suggested to turn the second *qui sunt undique* into *qui sunt ab apostolis*, taking this out from five words further on. The suggestion is plausible, it would carry out the idea of the beginning of our quotation very well, and it would clinch the papalism of the whole beyond possibility of cavil. "Those who are from the apostles" would be the Popes. But, so far, it is only conjecture.

[12] The antipapal interpretation of all this is that Irenaeus means that Rome is a great city; strangers go there from all countries, so by going to Rome you may find out what is believed by them, that is, in all countries. So J. Langen, *Gesch. der. röm. Kirche*, I, 171. F. W. Puller, who, as usual, finds this very passage a powerful argument *against* the papacy, expands this idea into seventeen pages (*The Primitive Saints and the See of Rome*, 3rd ed. [London: Longmans, 1914], 19–35). It is the exact opposite of what St. Irenaeus says. He says nothing about the greatness of the town; he says the *Church* of Rome has a mightier rule. He does not say that strangers go to the town but that every Church must agree with (or go to) the Roman Church. The tradition from the apostles is kept at Rome by those from all sides because of the mightier rule of this Church. That the guardian and teacher of the tradition

Church must agree with that of Rome (or go to Rome); because of this agreement the true tradition is kept in the other Churches. St. Cyprian (d. 258), in the text already quoted, where he says that the See of Peter is the chief Church whence priestly unity has come, adds that the African schismatics "had not considered that the Romans are those whose faith is praised by the apostle, to whom perfidy cannot have access".[13] One hundred and fifty-three Eastern bishops met in synod at Antioch in 379, under the presidency of the famous Meletius. In signing its acts they specially note their agreement with the faith of Rome:

> Here ends this letter or exposition of the Roman synod held under Pope Damasus, and sent to the East, to which all the Eastern Church, having held a synod at Antioch, agrees in the same faith; and all thus agreeing confirm the faith explained above, each one by his own signature.[14]

When Pope Damasus I (366–384) condemned the heresy that made the Holy Spirit less than God the Father and the Son (in 380), Sozomenus thus describes what happened:

> When this question was discussed and grew from day to day from love of debate, the Bishop of the city Rome, having heard of the matter, wrote to the Churches of the East that they must confess the consubstantial Trinity equal in honour and glory, as do the Western bishops. When he did this all were quiet, as the controversy was ended by the

---

is the Bishop of Rome is clear from what he has just said about "the series of her bishops down to us", and the list of Popes that follows our quotation.

[13] Ep. LIX, 14 (C.S.E.L. III, p. 683).

[14] PL XIII, 353.

judgment of the Roman Church; and this question at last seemed to be ended.[15]

Emperor Theodosius I (379–395) publishes a peremptory edict in 380:

> We command that all the people governed by our gracious rule live in that religion which the Divine apostle Peter handed down to the Romans, as the faith taught by him shows to this day, which, as is well known, the Pontiff Damasus professes, and Peter of Alexandria, a man of apostolic virtue.[16]

The Synod of Milan, about the year 389, states:

> But if they will not believe the teaching of the bishops, let them believe the oracles of Christ, let them believe the warning of angels who say: Nothing is impossible to God; let them believe the Apostles' Creed, which the Roman Church always keeps and preserves incorrupt.[17]

In 416 two synods were held in Africa, at Carthage and at Milevis, both against Pelagianism. Each submits its decrees to Pope Innocent I (401–417). He answers the synod at Carthage:

> Keeping the ancient tradition, remembering the discipline of the Church, you now strengthen your religion by consulting us, as much as when you made the decree. You have decided to refer to our judgment, knowing what is due to the Apostolic See. For we [the Pope], being placed here,

---

[15] HE VI, 22 (PG LXVII, 1346).
[16] PL XIII, 530; M. Rade, *Damasus, Bischof von Rom* (Tübinger: Mohr, 1882), 70–71. (Cod, Theod. XVI, 1–2.)
[17] Ambrosi, Ep. XLII, 5.

intend to follow the apostle, from whom the episcopate itself and all the authority of this name[18] is derived.[19]

To Milevis he writes:

> Rightly and properly you have consulted the judgment of the apostle's honour, I mean the honour of him who has, besides the things that are without, the care of all the Churches.[20] ... How is it you confirm this by your act, except that you know that we always send answers from the apostolic fount to those who seek them from all provinces? Especially whenever a question of faith is raised I hold that all our brothers and fellow-bishops should refer it to Peter only, that is, to the heir of his name and honor, as you have now done. For he can help all Churches in common throughout the whole world.[21]

Innocent speaks thus about a matter of faith. When this letter arrived at Milevis, St. Augustine spoke his famous words:

> Already two synods have sent to the Apostolic See concerning this affair [the Pelagian heresy]. The rescripts have

---

[18] The apostle in question is St. Peter. The idea that all episcopal authority comes from him, or from his see, occurs often in the Fathers. St. Cyprian: "Una ecclesia et cathedra una super Petrum Domini voce fundata" (Ep. LXIII, 5); "una ecclesia a Christo Domino nostro super Petrum origins unitatis et ratione fundata" (Ep. LXX, 3; cf. LXXIII, 7). Optatus: "in qua una cathedra unitas ab omnibus servaretur, ne ceteri apostoli singulas sibi quisque defenderent ... schismaticus qui contra singularem cathedram alteram collocaret. Ergo cathedra unica quæ est prima de dotibus" (II, 2–3). The episcopate is one body, of which the Pope is chief; in this sense the constitution of the Church is a monarchy. The three quotations in this footnote are given in English on, respectively, pages 58, 58 and 86.

[19] Innoc. I, Ep. XXIX, I (PL XX, 582–83).

[20] Innocent applies to St. Peter what St. Paul says of himself (2 Cor 11:28).

[21] Ep. XXX, 2 (PL XX, 590).

come from there, the cause is finished. Would that at last the error were finished, too.[22]

Again: "Concerning this matter all doubt had been removed by the letter of Pope Innocent of blessed memory."[23] Innocent's successor, Zosimus (417–418), says:

The tradition of the Fathers gives so much authority to the Apostolic See that no one dare contradict its judgment.... So great is our authority that no one may go back on our verdict.[24]

This is still about Pelagianism, a question of faith. Pope Celestine I (422–432) defined the Catholic faith in the matter of Pelagianism and Nestorianism; and he says: "The sanctions of the blessed and Apostolic See may not be violated."[25] The emperor Valentinian III (423–455) says:

We must defend the faith handed down by our fathers with all care; and we must keep the proper reverence due to the blessed apostle Peter incorrupt in our time also. Therefore the most blessed Bishop of the Roman city, to whom ancient right has given the authority of the priesthood over all, shall have his place, and power to judge about the faith and about bishops.[26]

St. Cyril of Alexandria (d. 444), in the matter of Nestorius, says to Pope Celestine I: "Since the old custom of the

---

[22] Sermo CXXXI (=de verb. apost. II), no. 10 (PL XXXIII, 758). This is the origin of the proverb: "Roma locuta est, causa finita est" (Rome has spoken, the case is finished).

[23] Contra duas Epist. Pelag. II, c. 3, no. 5 (PL XLIV, 574).

[24] Ep. XII, ad Aurelium ac cet., no. 1 (PL XX, 676).

[25] Ep. XXI, c. 11, no. 12.

[26] Ad Theodosium among St. Leo I's letters, Ep. LV (al. post XLVII, PL LIV, 859).

Churches persuades that questions of this kind should be communicated to your Holiness, I write, driven by necessity."[27] We have quoted St. Peter Chrysologus of Ravenna (d. c. 450).[28] His text applies most of all to this article, since he urges the heretic Eutyches to "attend obediently to what is written by the most blessed Pope of the Roman city; for St. Peter, who lives and reigns his own see, will help those who seek the truth."[29] This idea, that we must attend to what the Pope says in matters of faith because St. Peter, living in his successor, keeps that faith for all, is echoed at Chalcedon and is the very essence of the definition of Vatican I. So we will end our series of quotations with the famous cry that went up from the Fathers of Chalcedon after the dogmatic letter of St. Leo I had been read:

> This is the faith of the fathers; this is the faith of the apostles. We all believe so; the orthodox believe so. Anathema to him who does not so believe. Peter has spoken thus through Leo.[30]

Chalcedon in 451 brings us again to the end of our period. But it does not by any means bring us to the end of texts we could quote. Peter spoke through Leo when Monophysitism threatened the Church. Other storms were to threaten the People of Christ during the centuries that followed Chalcedon. Many times again the waves have threatened to wreck the ship; but always Christ was in her, always the man whom Christ appointed was at her helm. Through sixteen more centuries, Peter has spoken through a Leo, a

---

[27] Inter Ep. Cælestini I, VIII, no. 1 (PL L, 447).
[28] Cf. above, p. 77.
[29] *Ad Eutychen*, inter Ep. Leonis I, XXV, no. 2 (PL LIV, 741).
[30] Act. II (Harduin, II, 306).

Gregory, an Innocent, a Pius. Living and ruling on his throne by the Tiber, Peter still gives the faith to those who seek it. The present Pope will go to his account, as his predecessors have gone to theirs, but the voice of Peter will not die with him. For twenty centuries more, if the world last so long, Peter will live in his successors and will speak, when need arises, through them, till at the end the last Pope hands back to his Master the heavy burden of those keys that the first Pope received on the shore of the Lake of Galilee.

Are there no difficulties against our four theses from the first centuries? There are difficulties against every article of the faith. Many early Fathers would seem to have been Chiliasts (Millenarians); Justin Martyr seems to say that God the Father is greater than the Son; altogether a man could make a very pretty collection of apparent difficulties against the Holy Trinity from ante-Nicene Fathers.

There are fewer difficulties against the papacy than against most articles of the Catholic faith. The chief that occur in our period are, first, St. Cyprian's attitude in the matter of heretical baptisms. This we have already considered.[31] Then there is the case of Apiarius, the African priest who appealed to the Pope in 418. The African bishops resented this, because they thought his case ought to be tried by his own immediate authorities in his own country, an opinion with which no Catholic need find fault. The discussion then turned to the question of the canons of Sardica, which the Roman legates quoted as Nicene while the Africans could not find them in the copies of the acts of Nicea. All the same they were extremely respectful to the representatives of the Holy See, and St. Augustine promised that, since the legates said

---

[31] Cf. above, pp. 57–58.

so, they would observe the canons as Nicene, until they could verify them. Then there is the case of Meletius of Antioch (361–381), who was not recognized by Rome, the West and Egypt, because he was appointed by the Arians. But he was Catholic in faith, really, and was recognized by the Catholic bishops of the East. The dispute was an unfortunate one; it led to great trouble at Antioch, though it does not hinder the good relation of the friends of either party in the Church at large. Meletius was never out of communion with Rome, though he was not acknowledged there as lawful bishop of Antioch.[32] The Catholic friends of Meletius (St. Gregory of Nazianzos and St. John Chrysostom) made great efforts to reconcile his party completely with Rome. They succeeded in doing so finally in 398. But this is a long story.

Against one or two isolated difficulties of this kind, set the number of witnesses for the papal claims in the same period. It is impossible in this space to quote nearly all. I have chosen some prominent examples. By looking through Jaffé you will find among letters of Popes 166 instances of papal jurisdiction down to Leo I, all in matters of faith or nearly connected with faith.[33]

---

[32] See, for instance, H. Ryder, *Catholic Controversy*, 2nd ed. (London: Burns and Oates, 1881), pp. 59–60; F. Cavallera, *Le Schisme d'Antioche* (Paris: Picard, 1905).

[33] Here are the numbers, if anyone cares to look them up: 59, 66, 67, 70, 79, 82, 83, 84, 105, 106, 107, 109, 110, 111, 122, 125, 135, 136, 140, 188, 228, 232, 234, 235, 236, 251, 256, 260, 276, 281, 282, 283, 284, 293, 318, 319, 321, 322, 323, 329, 330, 342, 343, 352, 371, 372, 373, 374, 375, 376, 377, 380, 381, 385, 386, 387, 388, 392, after 396, 398, 402, 405, 412, 413, 416, 418, 420–33, 437–45, 447, 448, 449, 451–76, 478–83, 486, 487–96, 499, 500, 502–10, 514, 515, 517, 518, 520, 521, 524, 525–35, 537–42, 546–50.

An Anglican preacher once said that he found no particular difficulty against the papacy in practice. His difficulty is its historical justification in the early Church.[34] To the present writer the papacy seems one of the clearest and easiest dogmas to prove from that early Church. Theology would be an easier subject if everything could be shown to be the belief of the Church of Christ from the beginning as plainly as the papacy (of course, there are people who do not see that the early Church had bishops). If it is admitted that, in practice, the Church must have a general headquarters, and if we see that, as a matter of fact, she has had this from the beginning because Christ gave it to her, what difficulty against the papacy is left?

---

[34] N. P. Williams, *Our Case as against Rome* (London: Longmans, 1918), pp. 63, 87.

APPENDIX I

EXCERPTS FROM THE

Catechism of the Catholic Church[1]

816   "The sole Church of Christ [is that] which our Saviour, after his Resurrection, entrusted to Peter's pastoral care, commissioning him and the other apostles to extend and rule it.... This Church, constituted and organized as a society in the present world, subsists in (*subsistit in*) the Catholic Church, which is governed by the successor of Peter and by the bishops in communion with him."[2]

834   Particular Churches are fully catholic through their communion with one of them, the Church of Rome "which

---

[1] Quoted by permission of the publishers: Geoffrey Chapman in the U.K.; Veritas in Ireland. Numbers are paragraph numbers as in the original. Excerpts from the English translation of the *Catechism of the Catholic Church* for the United States of America copyright © 1994, United States Catholic Conference, Inc.—Libreria Editrice Vaticana. English translation of the *Catechism of the Catholic Church: Modifications from the Editio Typica* copyright © 1997, United States Catholic Conference, Inc.—Libreria Editrice Vaticana. Used with permission.

[2] *LG* [Vatican Council II, *Lumen gentium*] 8 § 2.

presides in charity." [3] "For with this church, by reason of its pre-eminence, the whole Church, that is the faithful everywhere, must necessarily be in accord." [4] Indeed, "from the incarnate Word's descent to us, all Christian churches everywhere have held and hold the great Church that is here [at Rome] to be their only basis and foundation since, according to the Savior's promise, the gates of hell have never prevailed against her." [5]

877   ... every bishop exercises his ministry from within the episcopal college, in communion with the bishop of Rome, the successor of St. Peter and head of the college. So also priests exercise their ministry from within the *presbyterium* of the diocese, under the direction of their bishop.

879   Sacramental ministry in the Church, then, is a service exercised in the name of Christ. It has a personal character and a collegial form. This is evidenced by the bonds between the episcopal college and its head, the successor of St. Peter, and in the relationship between the bishop's pastoral responsibility for his particular church and the common solicitude of the episcopal college for the universal Church.

880   When Christ instituted the Twelve, "he constituted [them] in the form of a college or permanent assembly, at the head of which he placed Peter, chosen from among

---

[3] St. Ignatius of Antioch, *Ad Rom.* 1, 1: *Apostolic Fathers*, II/2, 192; cf. *LG* 13.

[4] St. Irenaeus, *Adv. hæres.* 3, 3, 2: PG 7/1, 849; cf. Vatican Council I: DS 3057.

[5] St. Maximus the Confessor, *Opuscula theo.*: PG 91:137–140.

them." [6] Just as "by the Lord's institution, St. Peter and the rest of the apostles constitute a single apostolic college, so in like fashion the Roman Pontiff, Peter's successor, and the bishops, the successors of the apostles, are related with and united to one another." [7]

881   The Lord made Simon alone, whom he named Peter, the "rock" of his Church. He gave him the keys of his Church and instituted him shepherd of the whole flock. [8] "The office of binding and loosing which was given to Peter was also assigned to the college of apostles united to its head." [9] This pastoral office of Peter and the other apostles belongs to the Church's very foundation and is continued by the bishops under the primacy of the Pope.

882   The *Pope*, Bishop of Rome and Peter's successor, "is the perpetual and visible source and foundation of the unity both of the bishops and of the whole company of the faithful." [10] "For the Roman Pontiff, by reason of his office as Vicar of Christ, and as pastor of the entire Church has full, supreme, and universal power over the whole Church, a power which he can always exercise unhindered." [11]

883   "The *college or body of bishops* has no authority unless united with the Roman Pontiff, Peter's successor, as its head." As such, this college has "supreme and full authority over

---

[6] *LG* 19; cf. *Lk* 6:13; *Jn* 21:15–17.

[7] *LG* 22; cf. CIC [*Code of Canon Law*], can. 330.

[8] Cf. *Mt* 16:18–19; *Jn* 21:15–17.

[9] *LG* 22 § 2.

[10] *LG* 23.

[11] *LG* 22; cf. *CD* [Vatican Council II, *Christus Dominus*] 2, 9.

the universal Church; but this power cannot be exercised without the agreement of the Roman Pontiff." [12]

884   "The college of bishops exercises power over the universal Church in a solemn manner in an ecumenical council." [13] But "there never is an ecumenical council which is not confirmed or at least recognized as such by Peter's successor." [14]

885   "This college, in so far as it is composed of many members, is the expression of the variety and universality of the People of God; and of the unity of the flock of Christ, in so far as it is assembled under one head." [15]

891   "The Roman Pontiff, head of the college of bishops, enjoys this infallibility in virtue of his office, when, as supreme pastor and teacher of all the faithful—who confirms his brethren in the faith—he proclaims by a definitive act a doctrine pertaining to faith or morals. . . . The infallibility promised to the Church is also present in the body of bishops when, together with Peter's successor, they exercise the supreme Magisterium," above all in an Ecumenical Council. [16] When the Church through its supreme Magisterium proposes a doctrine "for belief as being divinely revealed," [17] and as the teaching of Christ, the definitions

---

[12] *LG* 22; cf. CIC, can. 336.

[13] CIC, can. 337 § 1.

[14] *LG* 22.

[15] Ibid.

[16] Ibid., 25; cf. Vatican Council I: DS 3074.

[17] *DV* [Vatican Council II, *Dei Verbum*] 10 § 2.

"must be adhered to with the obedience of faith." [18] This infallibility extends as far as the deposit of divine Revelation itself.[19]

892   Divine assistance is also given to the successors of the apostles, teaching in communion with the successor of Peter, and, in a particular way, to the bishop of Rome, pastor of the whole Church, when, without arriving at an infallible definition and without pronouncing in a "definitive manner," they propose in the exercise of the ordinary Magisterium a teaching that leads to better understanding of Revelation in matters of faith and morals. To this ordinary teaching the faithful "are to adhere ... with religious assent" [20] which, though distinct from the assent of faith, is nonetheless an extension of it.

2034   The Roman Pontiff and the bishops are "authentic teachers, that is, teachers endowed with the authority of Christ, who preach the faith to the people entrusted to them, the faith to be believed and put into practice." [21] The *ordinary* and universal *Magisterium* of the Pope and the bishops in communion with him teach the faithful the truth to believe, the charity to practice, the beatitude to hope for.

---

[18] *LG* 25 § 2.
[19] Cf. Ibid., 25.
[20] Ibid.
[21] Ibid.

APPENDIX 2

SUGGESTIONS FOR FURTHER READING

Aa.vv. The Petrine Ministry. In *Communio: International Catholic Review*, vol. 4, no. 4 (Winter 1998).

Balthasar, Hans Urs von. *The Office of Peter and the Structure of the Church*. San Francisco: Ignatius Press, 1986.

Congregation for the Doctrine of the Faith. "The Primacy of the Successor of Peter in the Mystery of the Church". In *L'Osservatore Romano*, November 18, 1998, pp. 5–6.

Garuti, Adriano. *Primacy of the Bishop of Rome and Ecumenical Dialogue*. Trans. Michael J. Miller. San Francisco: Ignatius Press, 2004.

Glazov, Gregory. "Vladimir Solovyov and the Idea of the Papacy". In *Communio: International Catholic Review*, vol. 24, no. 1 (Spring 1997): 128–42.

Horn, Stephan O. "The Petrine Mission of the Church of Rome: Some Biblical and Patristic Views". In *Communio: International Catholic Review*, vol. 18, no. 3 (Fall 1991): 313–21.

John Paul II. Encyclical letter, *Ut unum sint*. May 25, 1995, paragraphs 88–99.

Lubac, Henri de. *The Motherhood of the Church*. San Francisco: Ignatius Press, 1982. Part 2, "Particular Churches in the Universal Church", chapter 7, "The Service of Peter".

Nichols, Aidan. "Solovyov and the Papacy: A Catholic Evaluation". In *Communio: International Catholic Review*, vol. 24, no. 1 (Spring 1997): 143–59.

Pontificio Comitato di scienze storiche. *Il Primato del vescovo di Roma nel primo millennio: Ricerche e testimonianze: Atti del symposium storico-teologico, Roma, 9–13 ottobre 1989*. Libreria Editrice Vaticana, 1991.

Pottmeyer, Hermann J. "Why Does the Church Need a Pope?" In *Communio: International Catholic Review*, vol. 18, no. 3 (Fall 1991): 304–12.

Il Primato del Successore di Pietro: Atti del Simposio teologico, Roma, 2–4 dicembre 1996. Libreria Editrice Vaticana, 1998.

Ratzinger, Joseph. "Primacy, Episcopate, and Apostolic Succession". In *The Episcopate and the Primacy*, by Karl Rahner and Joseph Ratzinger, pp. 37–63. Freiburg and London: Herder and Nelson, 1962.

———. "The Papal Primacy and the Unity of the People of God". In *Church, Ecumenism and Politics*, Part 1, chapter 2. San Francisco: Ignatius Press, 2008.

———. "The Primacy of Peter and the Unity of the Church". Chapter 2 in *Called to Communion: Understanding the Church Today*. San Francisco: Ignatius Press, 1996.

Ray, Steven K. *Upon This Rock: St. Peter and the Primacy of Rome in Scripture and the Early Church*. San Francisco: Ignatius Press, 1999.

INDEX